Iqbal

MAKERS OF ISLAMIC CIVILIZATION

This series, conceived by the Oxford Centre for Islamic Studies and jointly published by Oxford University Press and I.B. Tauris, provides an introduction to outstanding figures in the history of Islamic civilization. Written by leading scholars, these books are designed to be the essential first point of reference for any reader interested in the growth and development of Islamic history and culture.

General Editor: F. A. Nizami
Series Manager: R. M. Ritter

Iqbal

Mustansir Mir

Oxford Centre for Islamic Studies

I.B. TAURIS

LONDON · NEW YORK

Published in 2006 by I.B.Tauris & Co. Ltd. and Oxford University Press India
in association with the Oxford Centre for Islamic Studies

I.B.Tauris & Co. Ltd.
6 Salem Road, London W2 4BU
175 Fifth Avenue, New York NY 10010
www.ibtauris.com

In the United States of America and Canada distributed by
Palgrave Macmillan, a division of St. Martin's Press
175 Fifth Avenue, New York NY 10010

ISBN 1 84511 094 3
EAN 978 1 84511 094 9

For all territories except South Asia

A full CIP record for this book is available from the British Library
A full CIP record is available from the Library of Congress

Library of Congress Catalog Card Number: available

Typeset in GoudyOlst BT
by Eleven Arts, Keshav Puram, Delhi 110 035
Printed in India by Ram Printograph, Delhi 110 051

For Raafia, Daniyal, and Khaldun

Acknowledgements

Dr M. Suheyl Umar, Director of the Iqbal Academy Pakistan, Lahore, very kindly arranged to ship from Pakistan many books on Iqbal; to him my debt is immense. Dr Farhan A. Nizami, Director of the Oxford Centre for Islamic Studies, Oxford, and the staff of the Centre were patient—very patient—and graciously accepted all the excuses offered to explain the delay in delivering the manuscript. To all of them my thanks! I had the benefit of receiving, from an anonymous reader, a very competent review, including many useful suggestions, for which I am grateful. My thanks also to Mr Robert Ritter of the Oxford Centre for Islamic Studies and Mr James Sacco of the Center for Islamic Studies at Youngstown, both of whom gave valuable help in editing the work. Any remaining inadequacies in the book can be safely imputed to me.

Iqbal's Texts Cited

POETRY

The Sheikh Ghulam Ali editions of Iqbal's Persian and Urdu poetry are used: *Kulliyyat-i Iqbal—Farsi* ('Collected Poetical Works of Iqbal—Persian'; Lahore, 1973) and *Kulliyyat-i Iqbal—Urdu* ('Collected Poetical Works of Iqbal—Urdu'; Lahore, 1973). All translations of the quoted material are my own. The page numbers given are those of the volumes of collected works rather than those of the individual works in the volumes. The poetical works are cited by the initials of their titles; these, together with the dates of publication, are given below:

Persian

AK: *Asrar-i Khudi* ('Secrets of the Self'): 1915; 2nd edn. 1918
RB: *Rumuz-i Bikhudi* ('Secrets of Selflessness'): 1918
PM: *Payam-i Mashriq* ('The Message of the East'): 1923
ZA: *Zabur-i 'Ajam* ('Psalms of Persia'): 1927
JN: *Jawid-Namah* ('The Poem of Eternity'): 1932
PCBK: *Pas Chih Bayad Kard Ay Aqwam-i Sharq?* ('What Must Now Be Done, O Nations of the East?'): 1936
AHf: *Armaghan-i Hijaz—Farsi* ('The Gift of the Hijaz'—Persian): 1938

Urdu

BD: *Bang-i Dara* ('The Sound of the Caravan Bell'): 1924
BJ: *Bal-i Jibril* ('Gabriel's Wing'): 1936
ZK: *Zarb-i Kalim* ('The Stroke of Moses'): 1937
AHu: *Armaghan-i Hijaz—Urdu* ('The Gift of the Hijaz—Urdu'):
1938

PROSE

The Development of Metaphysics in Persia (London, 1908) is cited
by the short title *Metaphysics*. *The Reconstruction of Religious Thought
in Islam*, ed. Saeed Sheikh (Lahore: Iqbal Academy Pakistan, 1996)
is cited by the short title *Reconstruction*; capital roman and arabic
numerals are used to refer to chapters—or lectures—and page
numbers, respectively (for example, IV. 91 means Lecture IV, page
91).

Letters of Iqbal to Jinnah (Lahore: Sh. Muhammad Ashraf, 1974;
first published 1942)
SWS: *Speeches, Writings and Statements of Iqbal*, ed. Latif
Ahmed Sherwani (Lahore: Iqbal Academy Pakistan, 3rd edn.
1977 (1995 reprint)
RMI: *Ruh-i Makatib-i Iqbal* (Urdu; 'The Essence of the Letters
of Iqbal'), ed. Muhammad Abdullah Qureshi (Lahore: Iqbal
Academy Pakistan, 1977)
SR: *Stray Reflections*, ed. Javed Iqbal (Lahore: Iqbal Academy,
rev. edn. 1992)

Preface

This book aims to introduce Muhammad Iqbal (1877–1938), a pre-eminent poet and philosopher of South Asia, to general readers in the English-speaking world. There is a respectable number of works on Iqbal in the English language, but very few of them set out systematically to acquaint the reader with the heart or substance of Iqbal's own writings. Within its limits, this volume tries to fill this gap. Based on a direct study of Iqbal's writings, it assumes no prior familiarity with Iqbal's works on the reader's part, and tries to bring into relief—in non-technical language and with substantial textual evidence—the principal contours of Iqbal's thought. It takes an expository and analytical approach to the subject. As such, it does not attempt to provide an account of the divergent critical constructions that have historically been placed on Iqbal's thought with a view to identifying Iqbal as a propounder or upholder of a certain philosophy or system of thought. Neither does it deal exhaustively with Iqbal's personal life or with his practical involvement in the social and political affairs of India. Finally, with a few exceptions, it does not discuss at length the question of Iqbal's sources and originality. Several works written on Iqbal (see Further Reading) will enlighten the reader on these and other matters. Two more clarifications are in order. First, I have approached Iqbal's writings synchronically. This, of course, leaves open the question of development and change in Iqbal's thought. Iqbal's views on certain issues—for example, those of nationalism and mysticism—did change significantly over time. But, even if we take the period of his stay in Europe (1905–8) as the turning point in the evolution of his thought, Iqbal's writings in the post-Europe period show remarkable consistency. A comparative study of Iqbal's talks, writings, and statements belonging to the years immediately following his return from Europe with those of the last few years of his life will show that Iqbal's thought on major issues of life did not change materially, though it certainly unfolded and grew in line with the inner logic of his fundamental convictions. Furthermore, there are grounds for presuming that the seeds of Iqbal's post-Europe thought were sown in his pre-Europe period. It must nevertheless be admitted that a detailed diachronic study of Iqbal's works is essential to understanding Iqbal's thought in all its rich variety.

Second, the book treats Iqbal's prose writings separately from his poetical writings: Chapters 2 and 3 deal with Iqbal's poetry, Chapters 4 and 5 with his prose. This approach might appear to be premised on the understanding that Iqbal's prose works are different in content and character from his poetical works. This, I should state clearly, is not my position. I believe that Iqbal's prose and poetical works, taken as a whole, are marked by a deep unity. A careful reader of even this short volume will not fail to notice a generic identity and a basic coherence between Iqbal's thought as expressed in his prose and his thought as expressed in his poetry. Unfortunately, it is not possible for me to elaborate on this matter any further here, but I intend to show in a subsequent study that the frequently raised question of the relationship between Iqbal's prose and poetry—with the attendant debate as to which of the two is to be accorded primacy for a general interpretation of Iqbal—is completely gratuitous. I have discussed Iqbal's poetry and prose in separate sets of chapters partly for convenience and partly because Iqbal's stature as a poet warrants a focused treatment of his poetical works. Furthermore, given the differences between the discursive nature of the prose medium and the rhetorical nature of the poetical medium, Iqbal

was able to treat certain issues at length only in prose, so it
made sense to reserve discussion of those issues in chapters devoted
to Iqbal's prose.

Here is an outline of the chapters:

Chapter 1 provides a brief life-sketch of Iqbal. It draws mainly
on *Zindah-Rud* ('The Living Stream' (see Further Reading)), the
Urdu biography of Iqbal by his son Javed Iqbal. An attempt is
made in the chapter to bring out the significance of the different
phases of Iqbal's intellectual development. The two concluding
sections of the chapter consist of notes on, respectively, Iqbal's
personality and his individual works. Chapter 2 presents, in several
sections, many of the major themes in Iqbal's poetry, though
without laying claim to exhaustiveness of treatment. Chapter 3
analyses some aspects of Iqbal's poetic art. Chapter 4 discusses
two of Iqbal's philosophical works in prose, *The Development of
Metaphysical Thought in Persia* and *The Reconstruction of Religious
Thought in Islam*, focusing on the latter. A summary of the chapters,
or lectures, of the *Reconstruction* is followed by a discussion of
several of the major foci of the book. The concluding section
compares the *Metaphysics* with the *Reconstruction*. Chapter 5 reviews
Iqbal's social and political thought as expressed in some of his
other prose works. In the interest of offering a manageable treatment
of the subject, I have used Latif Ahmed Sherwani's compilation
of Iqbal's writings, speeches, and statements as my main reference
(see Further Reading), and have only occasionally cited from Iqbal's
poetical works, which, to be sure, are an important source of
Iqbal's social and political views. (Chapter 2 partially atones for
this omission.) Chapter 6 offers observations on Iqbal's legacy.

Contents

1

Life, Personality, and Works

I. SIALKOT (1877–95)

Iqbal was born on 9 November 1877 at Sialkot, an old city in
the province of the Punjab in Pakistan. Some four and a half
centuries before his birth, his Brahmin ancestors in Kashmir
(northern India) had converted to Islam. In the late eighteenth
or early nineteenth century, when Afghan rule in Kashmir was
being replaced by Sikh rule, Iqbal's great-grandfather, or his sons,
emigrated from Kashmir to Sialkot. In his verses, Iqbal refers to
his Kashmiri origins and Brahmin ancestry. He weeps over the
suffering and misery of the people of the beautiful Kashmir Valley.
In one verse, he expresses wonder—and is also amused to think—
that, in spite of his Brahmin background, he became privy to mystic
insights that only the great Sufi masters possessed (ZA, 405).
Iqbal's father, Nur Muhammad, a tailor by profession, was a pious
individual with a mystic bent. Though he lacked a formal education,
he could read Urdu and Persian books and eagerly sought the
company of scholars and mystics, some of whom affectionately
called him an 'unlettered philosopher'. In a study circle held regularly
at his home, well-known Sufi classics were read, and this must
have been Iqbal's first introduction to Muslim mysticism. Wishing
to provide a religious education to his son, Nur Muhammad sent
4-year old Iqbal to a mosque where he learnt how to read the

Qur'an. Iqbal fondly relates several anecdotes to show how his views and attitudes were subtly but decisively influenced by his father's simple but deeply religious character. Iqbal's mother, though illiterate, was highly respected in the family as a wise, generous woman who quietly gave financial help to poor and needy women and arbitrated in neighbours' disputes. In a moving poem written at her death in 1914, Iqbal pays tribute to her compassion and wisdom.

Barely one year after joining the Qur'an school, Iqbal, now 5 years old, became a student of Sayyid Mir Hasan (1844–1929), a distinguished scholar of religion and literature who headed a *madrasa* (religious school) in the city. During their long association, Mir Hasan not only instructed Iqbal in the Islamic religious heritage, but also helped him cultivate a highly refined literary taste. Unlike many other Muslim scholars in India, Mir Hasan felt an urgent need for Muslims to acquire a European—which, in practical terms, meant secular—education in addition to a religious one. Their capture of Delhi in 1857 made the British *de jure* rulers of India, large parts of which had already been under their *de facto* control. Anger and frustration led many Muslims to reject everything that was associated with the ruling British—who had already blamed the Muslims for the 1857 Uprising. They accused the British of instituting policies prejudicial to their former dominant political and social position. In the field of education, the traditional Islamic disciplines of knowledge and the Persian and Arabic languages soon lost their pre-eminent position in society; by contrast, English and the modern arts and sciences gained in importance. As a consequence, the demand for scholars of Arabic and Persian diminished while the demand for scholars of English and modern disciplines of knowledge increased. Many Muslim religious leaders discouraged their followers from studying English—which they dubbed the language of the infidel usurpers of India—and from acquiring a modern education. Sir Sayyid Ahmad Khan (1817–98), educationist and reformer, disagreed with this view. He was convinced that the salvation of the Indian Muslims lay in accepting the fundamental change that had occurred in the real world.

Critical of the traditional Islamic educational system, which he termed stagnant and unproductive, he stressed the need for Muslims to study English and the European arts and sciences. Mir Hasan agreed with Sir Sayyid and supported his cause. He persuaded Iqbal's father to have Iqbal admitted to Sialkot's Scotch Mission College, where Mir Hasan was professor of Arabic. At this college, Iqbal obtained the Faculty of Arts diploma (1895)—the highest then offered by the college—which represented two years of education after high school. (The Scotch Mission College was later renamed Murray College, which still exists under that name.)

While at Scotch Mission, Iqbal, now 15 or 16 years old, started composing poetry, some of which was published. Like many other budding poets in India, he became a 'student by correspondence' of Mirza Dagh (1831–1905), a famous Urdu poet known as the 'Nightingale of India'. Dagh admired Iqbal's talent, and Iqbal always took pride in having been one of his students. In a poem he wrote on Dagh's death, Iqbal paid homage to Dagh's consummate artistic skills.

By the age of 18, Iqbal had acquired all that the city of Sialkot had to offer him. These early years engendered some of Iqbal's basic and characteristic attitudes, sympathies, and interests. His parents had given him a deep religious and mystical orientation, which he was to retain for the rest of his life. Iqbal's love for the Islamic scripture, the Qur'an, is well-known. The Qur'an, which he recited regularly, was a constant source of inspiration to him; indeed, Iqbal claims that his poetry is no more than an elucidation of the Qur'anic message. Iqbal's father once advised him to read the Qur'an as if it were being revealed to him direct from God, for only then, he said, would Iqbal truly understand it. This remark left an indelible impression on Iqbal's mind and determined his intellectual and emotional attitude towards the Qur'an. It later found expression in a memorable verse:

> Until the Qur'an is revealed to your own heart,
>   Neither Razi nor the author of the *Kashshaf* will untie its
>   knots for you.

(BJ, 370)

(Fakhr al-Din al-Razi (1150–1210) and Abu l-Qasim Mahmud al-Zamakhshari (1075–1144) were Qur'anic commentators, the latter's commentary bearing the title *al-Kashshaf*.) It has been suggested that Iqbal's choice of the subject of his doctoral thesis— Persian metaphysical thought—was indirectly influenced by his father. In apparent reference to his father's powerful spiritual influence on him, Iqbal used to say that he had not formed his view of life through philosophical investigation but had 'inherited' it, and that he used logic and reasoning only to support and vindicate that view.

The influence of Mir Hasan on Iqbal, too, was formative. Mir Hasan was a committed and enlightened scholar who not only instilled in Iqbal a profound love of the Islamic intellectual and literary heritage, but also introduced him to modern learning. It was through Mir Hasan that Iqbal came to know about Sir Sayyid. Iqbal's sympathy for Sir Sayyid's educational movement, even though Iqbal had serious reservations about the value of the European educational system it promoted, is well-known. Furthermore, if Iqbal's thought presents a unique synthesis of the Eastern and Western traditions of learning, and if that synthesis was expressed mainly through the medium of poetry at once serious and eloquent, then it was in Sialkot, and principally under Mir Hasan's guidance, that the first foundations of that synthesis were laid and the medium for its expression—poetry—chosen. In a poem written in praise of an Indian Muslim saint, Iqbal reverently talks about his intellectual and literary debt to his dear teacher. In 1922, when the British government decided to confer a knighthood on him, Iqbal made his acceptance of the honour contingent upon recognition of Mir Hasan's scholarship. Upon being asked what books Mir Hasan had written, Iqbal replied that he himself was the book Mir Hasan had authored. When Iqbal was knighted on 1 January 1923, Mir Hasan received the title of *Shams al-'Ulama'* (Sun of Scholars).

In 1893, Iqbal, then 16, married Karim Bibi, three years his senior. This was probably a hastily arranged match—and there are indications that Iqbal was against it, even though he deferred to his elders' decision in the matter. Karim Bibi bore him a son and a daughter. The strain in the couple's relations led to their separation, but Iqbal remained responsible for providing maintenance to Karim Bibi, who was to outlive him by eight years.

II. LAHORE (1895–1905)

In 1895, Iqbal moved to Lahore, beckoned by that city's greener pastures of learning. A major city of the Punjab, Lahore was known for its educational institutions and cultural activities. Iqbal secured admission to the famous Government College, where he spent four years, obtaining a BA in 1897—studying English, philosophy, and Arabic—and an MA in philosophy in 1899. Soon afterwards, he was appointed MacLeod Arabic Reader at Lahore's Oriental College, where he taught history, philosophy, and economics and worked on research and translation projects. He held this post intermittently until 1904. For a short period of time, he also served as Assistant Professor of English at Government College and at one other college in the city.

In Lahore, Iqbal's intellectual and literary talents blossomed. At Government College, he was exposed to the broad and vigorous tradition of European learning. Probably the most important influence on him was that of Sir Thomas Arnold (1864–1930), who had taught at Aligarh College before joining Government College in 1898. Quick to note Iqbal's abilities, Arnold coached him in several ways. Besides teaching Iqbal formally, he motivated him to undertake several research projects. During his tenure as MacLeod Arabic Reader, Iqbal, encouraged by Arnold, wrote a research paper on the Muslim mystic 'Abd al-Karim al-Jili's concept of the Perfect Man, abridged and translated into Urdu two English books (one on early English history, the other on economics), and wrote the first Urdu book on the principles of economics.

Lahore boasted several literary societies, which met regularly and provided opportunities for both well-known and upcoming poets to present their work before the general public. Iqbal quickly established his credentials as a fine poet. At first, he dealt with the conventional themes of Urdu poetry—love, suffering experienced on separation from the beloved, desire to reunite with the beloved—employing, to that end, the typical and popular Urdu *ghazal* (a love poem in lyrical verse; literally, love-talk with women). A little later, he chose and perfected *nazm* (narrative verse) as the principal form his poetry was to take. But even as a writer of *ghazals*, Iqbal's originality at times burst through the rigid framework of convention and his novel images gripped the audience's attention, winning him acclaim from noted poets and critics of the time.

Three developments at this stage of Iqbal's poetical career are significant. First, Iqbal's poetry shows an increasing influence of English poetry, as attested, for example, by his many nature poems. But instead of making a clean break with the Indian tradition of Persianate Urdu poetry, Iqbal draws on the literary resources of that tradition in dealing with the themes he had borrowed from English poetry. This was a new experiment, and was hailed as a breath of fresh air in the stifling atmosphere created by the styles of poetic composition then current in Urdu. A representative poem in this connection, 'The Himalayas', is briefly discussed in Chapters 2 and 3.

Second, influenced by English literature and European political thought, but also by the political developments within India, Iqbal begins to deal with themes of patriotism. His 'National Song of India' (*BD*, 83), which opens with 'Our country India is the best in the whole world', became immensely popular and was frequently sung in chorus, virtually like a national anthem, at schools and other gatherings across the country.

Third, Iqbal's poetry receives a new direction through his association with the Anjuman-i Himayat-i Islam (Society for the Support of Islam). The Anjuman was established in 1884 with a view to promoting the welfare of India's Muslims. Specifically, it offered financial support to students, established libraries and orphanages, and helped widows and poor people to stand on their own feet by giving them vocational training. It also set up a printing press to produce Islamic literature. The Anjuman's annual fund-raising events were attended by both distinguished national figures and the general public. At these meetings, speeches were made on important national and community issues and poems were read that appealed to religious sentiments. At the annual meeting of 1900, Iqbal read his poem 'The Orphan's Lament', which so moved the audience that he was asked to reread it. Thanks in part to Iqbal's poem, the Anjuman's fund-raising event that year was more than successful.

In Lahore, much more extensively than in Sialkot, Iqbal was exposed to the two traditions of Eastern and Western learning. This can be seen in the subjects he formally studied at Government College—Arabic, English, and philosophy. As in Sialkot, so in Lahore Iqbal found an able mentor: the precious stone discovered by Mir Hasan in Sialkot was polished into a glittering jewel by Arnold in Lahore. Under Arnold's affectionate patronage, Iqbal the poet now also became Iqbal the academic. Iqbal's studies, writings, and interests came to have remarkable diversity: he taught English, philosophy, history, and economics at several colleges and his writings included treatments of equally diverse subjects. Arnold motivated Iqbal to pursue higher studies in the West. Iqbal had probably already begun the process of intellectually synthesizing the Eastern and Western traditions. In the fertile soil of Lahore, the sapling of Sialkot had become a sturdy tree.

III. EUROPE (1905–8)

Arnold and Iqbal were highly appreciative of each other. When Arnold left for England in 1904, Iqbal wrote a touching poem in which he paid tribute to Arnold and expressed his resolve to follow him to England. With the financial assistance of his elder brother, Iqbal was able to realize his wish. In 1905, he arrived in Cambridge, entering Trinity College as a research scholar. In the early part of the twentieth century, Cambridge was a renowned centre of Arabic and Persian studies. Its luminaries included Reynold M. Nicholson, who later translated Iqbal's Persian poetical work *Asrar-i Khudi* into English (1920). At Cambridge, too, Iqbal met with the philosopher John McTaggart and attended his lectures on

Western thought. In the meantime, Iqbal also enrolled as a student of law at Lincoln's Inn in London. At Arnold's suggestion, furthermore, he registered as a doctoral student at Munich University. In June 1907, Iqbal obtained a BA from Cambridge. In November 1907, Munich University awarded him a PhD for his thesis on the development of metaphysics in Persia. In July 1908, Iqbal was admitted to the bar in London. In the same year, his doctoral thesis was published in London.

The European phase of Iqbal's life is notable for several reasons. During this period, Iqbal gave almost exclusive attention to his studies; never before or after was he to lead such an intense academic life. His devotion showed results—three degrees from three prestigious schools in three years was a remarkable feat by any standard. During his stay in Europe, Iqbal acquired a sound knowledge of the German language. He was already familiar with a variety of German works in translation, but now he was in a position to make a first-hand, in-depth study of the German philosophical and literary tradition. From this period onwards, references to German writers and their thoughts become more frequent in his works, and he begins to see himself playing in India a role similar to that played in Germany by Goethe, whom he greatly admired. The influence of German thought and literature thus seems to have served as a counterweight to that of English. It has been rightly suggested that Iqbal's interest in German literature was due partly to the phenomenon of the Oriental Movement, which represented the influence of Hafiz, Sa'di, Rumi, and other Persian poets on such writers as Herder, Rückert, Goethe, Schiller, and Heine.

Iqbal's preoccupation with his studies in Europe gave him few opportunities to compose poetry; the number of poems he wrote during this period is small, and he often had to decline requests to contribute poems to journals or newspapers in India. While in Europe, Iqbal, in fact, became sceptical of the need to write poetry at all: it seems that the opportunity for reflection and observation afforded by his stay in Europe compelled him to rethink the poet's role in society. With the Indian context in mind, he came to the conclusion that Urdu poetry, with its decadent themes and stock expressions, was totally inadequate to the higher task of nation-building. His association with the Anjuman-i Himayat-i Islam had already led to his composing of poems about India's Muslim community, and Iqbal seems to have become further convinced of the need to dedicate art to life. At the same time, he seems to have felt a certain inadequacy on his part—namely, that he lacked the ability to compose the type of poetry that was the need of the hour—and so he decided to stop writing poetry. When his friends opposed his decision, he agreed to defer to Arnold, who persuaded Iqbal to continue writing poetry.

In Europe, as in Lahore, Arnold played an important role in Iqbal's education and intellectual upbringing, and Iqbal's stay in Europe further strengthened the bond between them. It was Arnold who had arranged Iqbal's admission to Cambridge's Trinity College even before Iqbal had arrived in England. During his visits to London, Iqbal frequently stayed with Arnold, and when Arnold took six months' leave from the University of London, Iqbal substituted for him as professor of Arabic. It was at the recommendation of Arnold and others that Iqbal was exempted, during his doctoral studies, from fulfilling Munich University's residency requirements. Iqbal's doctoral thesis, upon publication, was dedicated to Arnold.

In Europe, Iqbal was able to make a close and critical study of Western civilization, on which he was to comment in much of his later work. While he admired certain aspects of that civilization, he was critical of its secular character and warned Muslims of the dangers of blindly imitating the West. In one of his verses, Iqbal says: 'The storm from the West has transformed Muslims into real Muslims' (BD, 267). Arguably, this observation applies first and foremost to Iqbal himself. During his stay in Europe, Iqbal underwent a major change in his view and estimation of nationalism. Before leaving for Europe, he had championed the cause of Indian nationalism and had worked for Hindu–Muslim unity. To him, loyalty to the country could coexist without any serious tension with one's commitment to one's religion. Consequently, he wrote poems in which he extolled Indian nationalism. In Europe, Iqbal witnessed at first hand the deep discord that jingoistic nationalism had caused among the major European powers and that, several years later, was to climax in World War I. Reflection on the European political situation led Iqbal to draw a distinction between the territorial and ethnic nationalism of Europe and the ideological universalism of Islam, and he eventually rejected the former in favour of the latter. This transformation in Iqbal's thought was to have far-reaching consequences for his poetry and thought.

IV. A SENSE OF MISSION (1908–38)

On his return to India in July, 1908 Iqbal set up legal practice in Lahore, where, for a while, he also taught philosophy at his alma mater, Government College. The struggle to establish himself financially made strenuous demands on his time. His married life, too, was far from happy. His first marriage had been unsuccessful. In 1910, he married Sardar Begum and, in 1913, Mukhtar Begum. The troubles in his personal life left him little time to pursue his literary interests, and, consequently, he wrote very little poetry in the first two or three years after his return from Europe. Increasingly, however, he took part in the activities of several social welfare organizations and became involved in different capacities with a number of educational institutions, including Punjab University and Mohammedan Anglo-Oriental College.

In 1911, the British government, acceding to Hindu political demands but causing grave disappointment to the Muslims, rescinded the 1905 partition of the Bengal province. The international scene, too, was depressing to Muslims. In 1911–12, Italy occupied Libya, France annexed Morocco, and several Balkan states attacked Turkey, divesting it of its East European possessions. The events at home and abroad created a sense of despair and helplessness in many sensitive Muslims, including Iqbal, whose life from now on is marked by a growing earnestness of purpose. In both prose and poetry, Iqbal now begins to address the plight of Muslims—not only in India but in the Islamic world at large—and, in the process, his philosophical and political ideas start to take a more definite shape. According to Iqbal himself, it was during his stay in England that he became preoccupied with the question of the decline of the historic Muslim community. This preoccupation is conspicuous in his subsequent literary output. Iqbal's Urdu poems had been appearing in periodicals, but his first book of poetry to be published—in 1915—was the Persian *Asrar-i Khudi*, which sought to offer a systematic treatment of core concepts of Iqbal's developed thought. Nicholson's English translation of the work (1920) introduced Iqbal in the West as a major literary and philosophical writer. Reviewing the English version, Herbert Read compared Iqbal to the famous American poet Walt Whitman (1819–92). In its scope and appeal, *Asrar-i Khudi* addresses the worldwide Muslim community. Several other Persian and Urdu collections of poetry followed. Becoming heavily engaged on the intellectual, educational, and social fronts, Iqbal gave public talks and academic lectures, wrote articles for journals and newspapers, assisted in the production of textbooks for students at school and college levels, and corresponded with many people, expressing, in many cases, his views on issues of national and international importance. His major philosophical work, *The Reconstruction of Religious Thought in Islam*, was published in 1934. He was invited to give the Rhodes lectures in 1934, but ill health prevented him from travelling to England.

The worldwide Muslim community—the *ummah*—became a major focus of Iqbal's attention in the post-Europe period. Iqbal, who had previously written 'National Song of India' (*BD*, 83), saying 'We are Indians, and India is our country' (the poem 'National Song of Indian Children' (*BD*, 87)) may also be mentioned in this connection), now wrote 'Islamic Community's Song', proclaiming 'We are Muslims, the whole world is our country'. Iqbal's concern for the uplift and well-being of the *ummah* is evident from his active involvement in several global Islamic causes. When the adventurer Bachchah-i Saqao captured Kabul in January 1929, ousting the ruler Amanullah Khan, Iqbal appealed to the Muslims of India to support the Afghan general Nadir Shah's campaign to defeat Bachchah-i Saqao. In September 1929, Iqbal presided over a large public gathering held to protest the growing Zionist influence, under British patronage, in Palestine. In his speech, he declared that Muslims put no trust in the investigative commission that Britain had intended to send to Palestine. In 1931, he represented the Muslims of India at a meeting of the World Islamic Congress held in Palestine. In 1931 and 1932, again representing India's Muslims, Iqbal participated in the London Round Table Conferences held to decide India's political future. In 1933, Iqbal and two of his friends travelled to Afghanistan at the invitation of Nadir Shah, who wished to consult them about Afghanistan's educational system.

In practice, of course, most of Iqbal's political activities were confined to India. In 1926, he was elected a member of the Punjab Legislative Council, a position he retained until 1930. He played an important role in determining the course of the Muslim League, which was to become India's largest Muslim political party. When the activities of militant Hindu proselytizing movements like the Shuddhi and Sanghatan led to Hindu–Muslim riots, Iqbal urged Muslims to follow the example of India's Hindu community and rely on themselves for their communal survival and progress. Formerly a supporter of the cause of Hindu–Muslim unity, Iqbal eventually became doubtful of the viability of the project, concluding that the Muslims of India must maintain their distinct religious and cultural entity. He also spoke of the need for a separate electoral system for Hindus and Muslims in India. In December 1930, at the annual meeting of the All-India Muslim League held at Allahabad, he delivered his famous presidential address in which he proposed the creation of a separate homeland at least for the Muslims of northwestern India. Although he did not live to see the creation of Pakistan in 1947, Iqbal is revered as its spiritual father—and as its national poet.

V. PERSONALITY

Iqbal used to discourage enquiries about his personal life and was not enthusiastic about having his biography written. Nevertheless, his works give us many glimpses of his personality. His biographies are another rich source of information about him, as is the record of his correspondence. In the autobiographical poem 'Piety and Impiety' (BD, 59–60), Iqbal tells of a neighbour, a religious scholar, who had heard that Iqbal, though well-versed in Islamic law and religion, was not exactly a pious individual; that he recited the Qur'an at dawn, but was also fond of music, which Islam forbids; that, under the influence of his philosophical training, he refused to regard Hindus as infidels; that he was not averse to associating with beautiful women; that he had Shi'ite leanings; that, in brief, Iqbal was 'a bundle of contradictions'. On accosting the scholar one day, Iqbal confessed that he himself did not know the truth about himself and that he wished someday 'to see Iqbal'. The poem concludes with this couplet:

> Even Iqbal does not know Iqbal—
> And this, by God, is no joke at all!

While the note of levity in the poem is unmistakable, the essential point made—namely, that Iqbal is a multifaceted personality—is correct.

Both by nature and training, Iqbal was a man of serious, reflective disposition. He had been brought up in an environment where religiosity and scholarship were prized. The child Iqbal sat patiently through sessions, held at his home, in which Islamic mystical classics, then beyond his understanding, were read by educated individuals. He had profound respect for the distinguished religious and mystical figures of Islamic history—in fact, of world history—as his poetry testifies.

There is no question about Iqbal's fundamental commitment in life. Both intellectually and emotionally, he was devoted to the ideals of Islam, which his early training had inculcated in him, and this devotion only grew with time, until his thought, as he himself remarks, became completely 'Qur'anicized'. But Iqbal was by no means a religious obscurantist. Several writers have commented on his acceptance of broad humanity. His closest friends included not only Muslims, but also Christians, Hindus, and Sikhs, and in his poetry he sang the praises of several famous ancient and modern non-Muslims.

One of the qualities that Iqbal admired is *faqr*. Literally 'poverty', the word, as used in Iqbal's poetry, represents an attitude of self-sufficiency and indifference to the trappings of power and fame (Iqbal also uses the word *dervishi* in roughly the same sense). Iqbal not only preached *faqr*, he also practised it. As a lawyer, he would not accept more than a few cases at a time, aiming to generate just enough income to tide him over for a month or two. When Sir Akbar Hydari, chief minister of Hyderabad, sent him a cheque for one thousand rupees, Iqbal, sensing that Sir Akbar had meant the gesture as a favour to him, returned the cheque and wrote a poem, citing his *faqr*—that is, his sense of dignity—as his reason for refusing to accept the offer.

Another quality that Iqbal admired is courage. Certainly, he himself had the courage of conviction. When he was knighted, one of his friends wrote to him, expressing his fear that Iqbal, now beholden to the British government, would no longer be able to speak his mind freely on issues of national importance. In his reply, Iqbal said that no power on earth could keep him from speaking the truth. Later events proved him right.

Iqbal had an affective disposition; it grew out of his sensitive relation to both faith and aesthetics. He wept as he recited the Qur'an; sometimes, his copy of the Qur'an, wet with his tears, had to be put out in the sun to dry. Powerful verse moved him similarly; in one case, he was so overcome by emotion on reading a set of verses that he almost fainted (RMI, 211). One of the high points of his emotional life was his visit to Cordova Mosque in Spain. The visit took him, in his own words, "to heights I had never experienced before" (RMI, 459). His poem 'Cordova Mosque' is reckoned by many as his masterpiece.

Iqbal had an eye for talent. He invited or encouraged a number of individuals to undertake different projects which he considered important. He persuaded Muhammad Ali Jinnah—later, founder of Pakistan—to return from England to India and provide political leadership to the country's Muslims. He invited Abu l-A'la Mawdudi—later, founder of the religious-political party Jama'at-i Islami—to undertake the reconstruction of Islamic jurisprudential thought along certain designated lines (the project did not take off because of Iqbal's death a short time later). He urged several disciples of Amir Mina'i to write a biography of the great Urdu poet, recommending that the work be written in English and published in a British journal or newspaper.

But Iqbal the serious intellectual also had a lighter side to his personality. He had a keen sense of humour and was capable of biting satire. Fine examples of humour and irony are found in several of his poetical works, as in *Bang-i Dara*, whose concluding section is entitled 'Zarifanah' (Humorous). One of the poems in this section (*BD*, 284) contrasts the business-like relationship between teacher and pupil in the modern, Western educational system with the loving, affectionate relationship between the two in the traditional, Eastern educational set-up. A wordplay on the Persian and Urdu word *dil* (heart) and the English word *bill* gives a sharp edge to the contrast. There was a time, Iqbal says, when the pupil felt like offering his *dil* to his teacher in gratitude for the latter's services, but, in these changed times, the pupil, after completing his studies, says to the teacher, 'May I have the *bill*, please!'

Iqbal was by no means an impious person, but he took particular delight in self-deprecation and often presented himself— quite convincingly to some—as one who had little regard for religious commandments. In this, he reflected, according to some, the influence of the *Malamatiyyah*, Muslim mystics who deliberately perform, as an aid to self-purification, acts that would bring them public reproach.

Iqbal had a fastidious literary taste. He was in the habit of meticulously revising his work, which often resulted in delayed publication, and he often destroyed the poems that, in his view, did not meet a certain standard of excellence. His mastery of Persian and Urdu is evidenced by his literary exchanges with scholars in which he defended his use of certain words and phrases by citing from great masters of the two languages in his support. He was, however, quick to accept and appreciate well-founded criticism.

Iqbal liked music and could play the guitar well. He had a melodious voice and was frequently asked to sing his poems at public gatherings. He ate sparingly. He would not eat beef—the reluctance probably being a carry-over, according to his son Javed Iqbal, of his Brahmin ancestors' reverence for the cow. Mango was his favourite fruit, and he liked turnip pickle (people of Kashmiri origin are known for their love of the vegetable). He was fond of collecting photographs of famous poets.

Iqbal became a legend within his lifetime, and his stature has only grown since. In Pakistan, at least, to cite a verse of Iqbal in support of one's view is practically to clinch the argument in one's favour. That was not always the case, though. On many occasions, he was criticized on account both of his views and of his diction. Iqbal was criticized by many. He was attacked for accepting a knighthood, for writing poems to celebrate or commemorate certain occasions (like the coronation of George V or the death of Queen Victoria), for refusing to support the civil-disobedience movement against the British rulers, and for addressing God in a seemingly audacious manner in his poetry. But Iqbal has also had his defenders, including some of the best-known religious scholars and literary writers, and they have mounted a spirited defence of Iqbal against the charges brought against him. Iqbal lived a simple, dignified, and principled life. His biographers point out that, during most of his life—especially his last few years, when he was at the height of his fame—he lived in straitened circumstances, and that the British would have been only too happy to patronise him and give him financial support had he asked for it. He was aptly called 'the poorest knight'.

VI. WORKS

Iqbal wrote with great facility in three languages—Urdu, Persian, and English—and produced works in all three. He wrote prose

in English, poetry in Persian, and both prose and poetry in Urdu.
A brief introduction to his books, in order of publication, follows:

Poetical Works

Asrar-i Khudi (*Secrets of the Self*; Persian; 1915). Drawing on the
religious, spiritual, and literary sources of Islam, Iqbal in this work
offers a detailed statement of his philosophy of selfhood, illustrating
the main elements of that philosophy with stories and anecdotes.
In the poem, Iqbal is conscious of his role as the bearer of a
prophetic message to the Muslims of his age. The essence of
that message is cultivation of dynamic human personality through
action, struggle, and acceptance of life's challenges. In the poem,
Iqbal acknowledges the influence of Rumi, who became a constant
source of inspiration and guidance. The poem also illustrates Iqbal's
conviction that the proper function of art is ennoblement of life.

Rumuz-i Bikhudi (*Mysteries of Selflessness*; Persian;1918). This
work is a companion volume to *Asrar-i Khudi*. If *Asrar-i Khudi*
is concerned with developing the selfhood of the individual,
Rumuz-i Bikhudi deals with the role and function of the individual
in society. Individuals, in Iqbal's view, can develop their full potential
only within society and only when they contribute to the larger
objectives of the community to which they belong. In a very real
sense, one can speak of a communal self just as one speaks of
the individual self.

Payam-i Mashriq (*The Message of the East*; Persian; 1923). In
the Preface to *Payam-i Mashriq*, Iqbal says that he was motivated
to compose *Payam-i Mashriq* by Goethe's *West-Östlicher Divan*.
After quoting Heine to the effect that Goethe's *Divan* represents
a spiritually weak West's attempt to draw strength and vitality
from the East, Iqbal says that *Payam-i Mashriq* aims to highlight
the moral and religious verities that bear on the character-training
of individuals and nations. The work also has a more immediate,
practical goal, for Iqbal observes that the conditions of India in
his day bear some resemblance to the conditions of Germany in

Goethe's age. *Payam-i Mashriq* deals with a variety of philosophical, political, and literary themes and subjects, and represents some of the highest points of Iqbal's poetic art.

Bang-i Dara (*The Sound of the Caravan Bell*; Urdu; 1924). Divided into three parts, with the first part ending in 1905 and the second in 1908, this book helps us to understand, as no other book of Iqbal's does, several aspects of the evolution of his thought and orientation. Part I includes some memorable nature poems, several poems for children—some of them translations or adaptations of Western originals—and a few patriotic poems. Sir Abdul-Qadir's Introduction provides useful background about the work.

Zabur-i 'Ajam (*Persian Psalms*; Persian; 1927). In one of his letters, Iqbal summarises the contents of this four-part work: the first two parts present, respectively, man in conversation with God and man commenting on the world of man; the third part offers responses to a series of philosophical questions raised in a poem by a Muslim mystic of the thirteenth and fourteenth centuries; and the fourth part discusses the impact of slavery on a nation's religion and culture. In general usage, however, the title *Zabur-i 'Ajam* refers to the first two parts, each of the last two parts having acquired an almost independent status as a poem. Both for profundity of thought and exquisiteness of diction and style, *Zabur-i 'Ajam* occupies a distinctive place in Iqbal's poetical corpus.

Jawid-Namah (*The Poem of Eternity*; Persian; 1932). Often compared to Dante's *Divine Comedy*, *Jawid-Namah* recounts Iqbal's spiritual journey, under Rumi's guidance, through a series of heavenly spheres, the journey ending with Iqbal reaching God's presence and holding a dialogue with God. All the major philosophical and other issues that Iqbal had dealt with in his writings are here treated from a unified perspective, forming a coherent scheme of thought. In this work, Iqbal discusses a number of thought-systems, movements, and personalities of ancient and modern history.

Musafir (*Traveller*; Persian; 1934). This poem contains Iqbal's reflections on Afghanistan's history during his visit to the country at the invitation of Nadir Shah, and expresses his hope that the brave and freedom-loving Afghans will, taking guidance from the Qur'an, revive the glory of Islam.

Pas Chih Bayad Kard Ay Aqwam-i Sharq? (*What Must Now be Done, O Nations of the East?* Persian; 1936). This poem aims to shock the world's Muslims into reality after Italy's invasion of Abyssinia in 1936. Though focused on political issues of the time, the poem develops several of the religious and philosophical themes found in Iqbal's other works.

Zarb-i Kalim (*The Stroke of Moses*; Urdu; 1936). Called by Iqbal 'a declaration of war against the present age', *Zarb-i Kalim* is highly critical of certain aspects of modern—more specifically, Western—politics, culture, and lifestyle. The book inveighs against both Muslim societies and the world at large for their failure to live up to high, noble principles; it also calls upon its readers to act to change the world.

Armaghan-i Hijaz (*The Gift of the Hijaz*; Persian and Urdu; 1938). Published posthumously, *Armaghan-i Hijaz* has two parts, one Persian and one Urdu. It consists mostly of quatrains that sum up Iqbal's views and ideas on a variety of subjects. The Urdu section contains the celebrated 'Iblis's Advisory Council', in which Iblis, or Satan, after listening to his advisors, who are apprehensive about the rise of new philosophies and movements in the world, tells them that Islam is the only real threat to Satanic rule.

Prose Works

'Ilmu'l-Iqtisad (*Political Economy*; Urdu; 1903). *'Ilmu'l-Iqtisad*, Iqbal says in the Preface, is based on 'several well-known and authentic books' and contains, in places, his 'personal opinions' as well (p. 32). After stating the nature and method of economics, the book treats the subjects of production, exchange, distribution, and consumption of wealth, in that order. In this book, Iqbal coined Urdu equivalents for a number of English economic terms. Iqbal argues that a nation's economic development is bound up

with the education of the masses. Several economic ideas presented in his later prose or poetical writings hark back, directly or indirectly, to *'Ilmu'l-Iqtisad.*

The Development of Metaphysics in Persia (English; 1907; published 1908) was the title of the doctoral thesis that Iqbal presented to Munich University. Though written almost a century ago, it is still of considerable interest to the scholar, and several portions of it are accessible to the general reader.

Stray Reflections (edited by Javed Iqbal; English; 1910). This is a notebook containing Iqbal's 'odd jottings based on his impressions of the books he was reading at that time, his thoughts and feelings about the environment in which he lived, and reminiscences of his student days' (editor's Introduction, p. 1). Considering that Iqbal made these jottings in the span of a few months in the year 1910, one is struck both by young Iqbal's range of intellectual and literary interests and by his perceptive comments and evaluations of many writers, ideas and theories, institutions, and historical events and movements. A number of ideas presented herein were later developed by Iqbal, so that *Stray Reflections* might be called a springboard for his mature philosophical thought.

The Reconstruction of Religious Thought in Islam (English; 1930; expanded Oxford edn., 1934). This work originally consisted of six lectures that were delivered in several Indian cities in 1929; a seventh lecture, written at the request of London's Aristotelian Society, was later added. Many consider it the most important philosophical work of modern Islam.

Iqbal published a number of journal and newspaper articles on various subjects, issued statements on many important occasions, and engaged in correspondence with people from practically all walks of life. Latif Ahmed Sherwani's *Speeches, Writings and Statements of Iqbal* (Lahore: Iqbal Academy Pakistan, 3rd edn. 1977) is a representative compilation of such writings, though it does not aim to offer a selection of Iqbal's correspondence. Of particular importance in the volume are the following: the presidential address delivered at the annual session of the All-India Muslim League in 1930 (Part I); the essays 'Islam as a Moral and Political Ideal', 'The Muslim Community—a Sociological Study', 'Political Thought in Islam', 'Islamic Mysticism', and 'Position of Women in the East' (Part II); the open letter to Jawaharlal Nehru, 'Islam and Ahmadism' (Part III); and letters or statements numbered 3, 4, 17, 19, 25, 30, 31, 34, and 35 (Part IV). Sherwani's volume should be supplemented by B. A. Dar's collection, Letters and Writings of Iqbal (Lahore: Iqbal Academy Pakistan, 2nd edn. 1967), which also contains Iqbal's outline for a planned book, 'Introduction to the Study of Islam'. Finally, the Letters of Iqbal to Jinnah (Lahore: Sh. Muhammad Ashraf, 1974; first published 1942) provides an important elaboration of some aspects of Iqbal's political thought.

An English manuscript of Iqbal about a poet-philosopher of Muslim India, Mirza Abdul-Qadir Bedil (d. 1721), has been edited, with an Urdu translation, by Tehsin Firaqi. The work, Bedil in the Light of Bergson (Lahore: Iqbal Academy Pakistan, 1995; first published 1988) is a highly interesting study in comparative philosophy and literature and awaits study by Iqbal scholars.

2

Major Themes of Poetry

Iqbal's poetry has an extraordinary variety of themes. A randomly drawn list would include religion and politics, reason and intuition, freedom and determinism, life and death and their mysteries, individual and society, Eastern and Western cultures, art and literature and their role in society, knowledge and education, master and slave and their psychology, natural phenomena, and distinguished figures of world history. A more detailed look at the individual themes will illustrate the thematic variety even more sharply. Here, for example, is a partial list of the famous individuals Iqbal has written about in his poetry:

- Rama (ancient Hindu figure who typifies the ideal person)
- Abu Bakr (Muhammad's companion and first caliph of Islam, d. 634)
- Tariq ibn Ziyad (young Muslim general who initiated the conquest of Spain in 711)
- 'Abd ar-Rahman I (founder of Umayyad rule in Muslim Spain, d. 788)
- Abu l-'Ala al-Ma'arri (Syrian Arab poet and prose writer, d. 1058)
- Afdal al-Din Khaqani (Persian poet, d. 1199)
- Jalal al-Din Rumi (Persian poet, d. in Qonya, Anatolia, 1273)
- Guru Nanak (founder of the Sikh faith in India, d. 1539)
- William Shakespeare (English poet and playwright, d. 1616)

- Abdul-Qadir Bedil (Indian Muslim poet who wrote in Persian, d. 1720)
- Napoleon Bonaparte (French general and emperor, d. 1821)
- Johann Wolfgang von Goethe (German poet, dramatist, and novelist, d. 1832)
- Sandor Petöfi (Hungarian poet-soldier, d. 1849)
- Auguste Comte (French philosopher, d. 1857)
- Mirza Asadullah Khan Ghalib (Indian Urdu poet, d. 1869)
- Karl Marx (German socialist thinker, d. 1883)
- Jamal al-Din al-Afghani (modern Muslim thinker-activisit, d. 1898)
- Friedrich Nietzsche (German thinker, d. 1900)
- Leo Tolstoy (Russian novelist and thinker, d. 1910)
- Vladimir Lenin (Russian Bolshevik leader, d. 1924)
- Mustafa Kemal (founder of modern Turkey, d. 1938)
- Henri Bergson (French philosopher, d. 1941)
- Benito Mussolini (Italian dictator, d. 1945)
- Albert Einstein (German-born physicist, d. 1955)

But perhaps more impressive than the thematic variety of Iqbal's poetry is the function which that poetry performs. Quite apart from the question of whether the East and the West are more different than alike, it is probably correct that, generally speaking, poetry has been used in the East, much more so than in the West, not only to communicate personal feelings but also to present systems of thought. This is illustrated by much of high poetry in the major Islamic languages, and Iqbal's poetry falls within that literary tradition. Practically all of Iqbal's poetical works can be studied, at one level or another, as statements or expositions of a certain philosophical viewpoint. The philosophical nature of Iqbal's poetry has given rise to a debate: is Iqbal a poet or a philosopher? The question arises because of an inability to fit Iqbal neatly into one of the existing, pre-labelled pigeonholes—or, what amounts to the same thing, because of a failure to appreciate the distinctive character of his work. The so-called discrete strands of poetry and philosophy are not very discrete in Iqbal. Few other

Muslim writers have succeeded so well in integrating the two strands—or rather, in producing work that, viewed from one angle, is profound philosophy and, viewed from another, is poetry of the highest literary merit. A study of Iqbal's poetical works will provide evidence of Iqbal's masterful use of the medium of poetry to convey philosophic thought. A review of selected themes of his poetry in this chapter, complemented by a look at aspects of his poetic art in the next, will give some idea of how Iqbal achieves that goal.

I. NATURE

Iqbal wrote a number of poems specifically about nature; in many others, nature serves as background or forms a subsidiary theme. Four levels of Iqbal's engagement with nature may be distinguished.

First, some of Iqbal's poems celebrate the simple beauty of nature, like 'The Cloud' (BD, 91), which describes the movement of clouds and the onset of rain, or 'An Evening' (BD, 128), a description of a quiet evening along the river Neckar in Heidelberg. To this category also belong poems that go a little beyond simple description, extolling the purity of the natural environment or, in some cases, exploring the mythical dimension of nature. A good example is 'The Himalayas', which opens Bang-i Dara. One of his first poems to be published, it prefigures Iqbal's deep and abiding interest in nature. Its opening lines speak of the agelessness of the Himalayas, comparing the mountain range favourably with Mount Sinai, where, according to Qur'an 7. 142, God manifested Himself at Moses' request:

> O Himalayas,
> Bulwark of the kingdom of India,
> The skies bend down to kiss you on the forehead!
> You show no signs of age:
> The revolving days and nights have ever found you young.
> For the Moses of Sinai there was but one epiphany;
> To the discerning eye you are an epiphany incarnate.

(BD, 21)

According to legend, Adam, after his expulsion from the Garden of Eden, first landed on the Himalayas. Since the Himalayas remember those days of man on earth, Iqbal is eager to hear from the mountain range the story of the age when human beings lived a simple, unaffected life. The implied criticism of 'civilization' in the following lines will not be missed:

> O Himalayas, tell us the story of the times
> When man's first parents first dwelt in your hem.
> Do tell of that simple life
> That was untainted by the rouge of affectation.
> O imagination, show us again those days and nights—
> Run back in your tracks, O revolving time!
>
> (BD, 23)

This category of poems may be further enlarged to include poems that celebrate the sensible beauty of nature but, at the same time, invite the reader to discover a deeper meaning in nature. An example is 'The Season of Spring' (PM, 261–4), whose six stanzas of seven lines each chart a progression from vivid descriptions of garden scenes to brief reflective remarks on life.

Second, nature is a congenial companion, its restful lap providing escape from the humdrum of ordinary existence and from the troubles and worries of life. This 'far from the madding crowd' motif is found in an early poem, 'A Wish'. Iqbal wishes to have 'a small hut at the foot of a hill', where

> I am free from worry, and can live in seclusion,
> With the thorn of world pain removed from my heart;
> Where the chirping of birds gives the pleasure of music,
> And the fountain's murmurings are like an instrument playing;
> Where the rose-bud, cracking open, delivers a message from someone;
> The little wine-cup displaying to me the whole world;
> Where my arm is my pillow, and the grass my bed,
> And where solitude puts company to shame;
> Where the nightingale would find my face so familiar
> That his little heart would have no fear of me;
> Where, with lush plants lined up on both sides,
> The stream's limpid water takes pictures;

Where the view of the mountain is so charming
That the water itself jumps up in waves to take a look;
Where the green grass lies asleep in the earth's lap,
And the water glistens as it moves through the shrubs;
Where the rose branch bends down to touch the water,
As if some beauty were looking in the mirror;
Where, when the sun adorns the bride of evening with henna,
The robe of every flower is tinged with rouge of a golden hue.

(BD, 47)

Third, nature serves as a spur to serious reflection. Study of the patterns of nature yields definite lessons for human beings. In 'The Morning Sun', Iqbal wishes to emulate the sun, which, as it looks down from the heavens, treats alike 'high and low'. Iqbal, too, would like to view and treat all human beings equally, rising above the artificial barriers dividing humankind:

In your eyes the high and the low are one;
That is the kind of vision I desire.
I wish my eyes were moist from the sorrow felt for others,
I wish my heart were free from the distinctions of faith and creed.

(BD, 49)

And sometimes nature serves Iqbal as a focal point of reflection on his own situation or on the human situation in general. In 'The River Wave', the wave speaks of its restlessness and then offers an explanation for it: it longs to reunite with the sea, from which, as a wave, it has been separated. The poem deals with one of Iqbal's favourite themes—namely, that separation from one's source or object of love gives rise to pain and restlessness, whereas reunion with it gives joy and contentment—a theme that is also prominent in Sufi literature. Here is the complete poem, which, like several others, can be said to have an autobiographical element:

My impatient heart keeps me restless;
To toss and turn, like quicksilver, is very life to me.
Wave is my name, the sea is ankle deep to me,
And the ring of the vortex will never be my chains;

Like the wind my steed moves through the waters,
My dress never caught on the prickly bone of a fish.
Sometimes, attracted, I jump up to the full moon;
Sometimes, in passion, I smash my head against the shore.
I am a traveller, and am in love with my destination.
Why am I restless? Let someone ask that of my heart.
I shy away from the distressing straits of the river;
I am distraught because I pine for the vast sea.

(BD, 62)

In 'The Moon', Iqbal first notices a few likenesses between the moon and himself: both live a solitary existence; both are in search of a destination; and both are smitten by love—the moon by love of the sun, Iqbal by love of God's eternal beauty. But, upon further reflection, Iqbal realizes that the two are very different, too:

And yet, O shining moon,
You are different from me,
And I am different from you!
The heart that feels the pain
Is a different heart indeed.
Though I am all darkness and you are all light,
Yet you are far removed from the station of awareness.
I know the purpose of my life—
And this is a radiance your face does not have.

(BD, 79)

Comparison with nature, in other words, reveals the human beings' distinction, aiding them in establishing their identity and determining the nature of their special calling in life. One of the most intriguing poems of Iqbal in this category is 'Solitude' (PM 288), which I have discussed in detail elsewhere (see Mir, *Tulip in the Desert*, pp. 43–5, 49–50).

Fourth, nature serves as a foil for drawing out man's potential. Nature is God's unfinished business—like a rough-hewn rock awaiting a sculptor's hand to chisel a masterpiece from it. In perfecting what is imperfect in nature, human beings fulfil their proper role in the world, discharging, at the same time, their role as God's colleagues. The short poem 'A Dialogue Between God and Man', a polemic between God and man, makes a serious point (for a translation of the poem, with commentary and notes, see Mir, *Tulip in the Desert*, pp. 11, 20). God accuses man of putting to evil use the benign natural objects He has created:

> From the earth I produced pure iron,
> But you made from that iron sword, arrow, and gun.

In his carefully worded response, man does not offer a direct rebuttal of the charge, but rather points to his enhancement of an otherwise crude and undeveloped nature:

> You made deserts, mountains, and valleys;
> I made gardens, meadows, and parks.
> I am one who makes a mirror out of stone,
> And turns poison into sweet, delicious drink.

(PM, 284)

It is a short step from nature as foil to nature as object of conquest. The fourth level of Iqbal's engagement with nature includes, therefore, man's endeavour to gain control of nature. In the remarkable poem *Taskhir-i Fitrat* (Conquest of Nature) in *Payam-i Mashriq*, Adam, after having been seduced by Satan—who had claimed to be lord of nature—now resolves to master nature, so that he may outsmart Satan—who claims to have command of the elements of nature—and bring him to his knees (for a translation and study of the poem, see Mir, *Tulip in the Desert*, pp. 21–4). Incidentally, man's conquest of nature is not always accompanied by illumination of the dark alleys of the human mind itself, and this 'dissonance' occasions irony, which does not escape Iqbal's notice (see next section).

II. THE HUMAN SITUATION

To Iqbal, human beings are a remarkable species. In 'The Story of Adam' (*BD*, 81–2), Iqbal offers a succinct summary of human achievements in history. Beginning with the departure of Adam from the Garden of Eden, the poem weaves its way through several ages and several lands. The many distinguished persons alluded to in the poem include not only prophets (Moses, Elijah of Tishbe, Jesus, and Muhammad), but also ancient Greek thinkers, the Italian astronomer Galileo (d. 1642), the English physicist Isaac Newton (d. 1727), the English scientist Michael Faraday (d. 1867), and the German scientist Wilhelm Röntgen (d. 1923). The poem eulogises those courageous religious personalities who ceaselessly struggled and suffered to bring spiritual illumination to the world, and also those fearless spirits of the Renaissance who championed the cause of science and knowledge in the face of religious obscurantism and oppression.

Just as human talent and courage evoke Iqbal's admiration no matter where found and in whom, so the human situation, again without regard to land or people, draws his attention and elicits a response from him. Iqbal is painfully aware of the transient nature of all that is good and beautiful: 'The thorn lives to reach old age, but the rose, as soon as it reaches the stage of youth, perishes' (PM, 198). He laments that human beings possess only limited ability to pursue their limitless ambition: 'The heart longs to see, but the eyes are bereft of vision' (BD, 216). And he asks God if, by involving the human being—'this handful of dust'— in this dilemma, He does not mean to play a practical joke:

> This handful of dust,
> This fiercely blowing wind,
> And these vast, limitless heavens—
> Is the delight You take in creation
> A blessing or an oppression?
>
> (BJ, 300)

Nor is this the only irony of human life. Humans, while they have had a great career as far as conquering the external world of nature is concerned, have a rather dismal record when it comes to solving their personal and social problems:

He who discovered the orbits of the stars
Failed to travel in the world of his own thought;
He was so lost in the maze of his philosophy
That, to this day, he is unable to tell his gain from his loss.
He who took the sun's rays prisoner
Failed to light up the dark night of his own life.

(ZK, 531)

And so one can justifiably say that Adam, a revealer of secrets, is 'a secret himself' (PM, 209).

In the end, however, Iqbal puts his trust in the human being, a trust vindicated by the contribution that human beings have made in turning this world into a beautiful place. Addressing God, Iqbal purports to speak on behalf of humankind:

Have you not seen that we, whose origin is dust,
Have so beautifully decked out this world of dust?

(AHf, 900)

By assigning value to everything, and by transforming the world for the better, the human being attains to a very high status:

God created the world, but Adam made it better—
Adam, perhaps, is God's co-worker.

(PM, 198)

Iqbal was fascinated by the idea that humans, though made of earth, are yet possessed of a certain element that impels them to break free of their earthly limitations and engage in a ceaseless search for loftier goals. It is hard to say what the origin of that element is, though it is certain that it is non-material in character. Here, for the sake of convenience, we will call it 'spirit' or 'mind'. The subsistence of the non-physical in the physical, of mind in matter, or of soul in body—the presence of the wine in the tumbler, as Iqbal puts it in the following poem—is a mystery. But a greater mystery is that the non-physical element drives the physical body, filling it with an 'ardent longing', with the 'pain of quest', and with the 'obsession' to rise to galactic heights. Is Iqbal's question about the origin of the non-physical element in the human being a serious or a rhetorical question? Given Iqbal's preoccupation with the idea—here and elsewhere—the first possibility cannot be completely excluded. Here is the poem:

The ardent longing in our hearts—
Where does it come from?
Ours is the tumbler, but the wine within—
Where does it come from?

I know that this world is mere dust,
And that we, too, are but a handful of dust.
But this pain of quest that runs through our being—
Where does it come from?

Our glances reach the neckline of the Galaxy;
This obsession of ours, this tumult and clamour—
Where does it come from?

(ZA, 397)

III. KHUDI

Iqbal is often called the philosopher of *khudi* (selfhood). The question 'What does Iqbal mean by *khudi?*' raises complex issues. We will attempt only a brief answer.

In a metaphysical sense, *khudi* is the ultimate ground of all existence. It is a primordial force—in *The Reconstruction of Religious Thought in Islam* (see Chapter 4), Iqbal calls it the Ultimate Reality or the Absolute Ego, whose personal name is Allah or God. This force, which we may call Divine *khudi*, through self-assertion or self-manifestation, gives rise to the phenomenal world:

Visible existence is one of the imprints of *khudi*;
Everything you see is one of the secrets of *khudi*.
Khudi, when it woke itself up,
Brought forth this world of presumed existence.

Concealed in it are a hundred worlds;
By affirming itself it gives rise to other-than-itself.

(AK, 12–3)

Why does Divine *khudi* create other-than-itself out of itself,
sowing 'seeds of dissension'? So that, through the ensuing conflict,
it may become aware of its own power, and so that the resulting
competitive pursuit may lead to the creation of new values and
higher ideals (AK, 13).

Just as it is in the nature of Divine *khudi* to reveal itself, so
it is in the nature of every individual existent to express itself,
since every existent has a *khudi* of its own. In fact, a thing truly
partakes of existence only insofar as it possesses the urge to express
itself—that is, only insofar as it possesses *khudi* (AK, 14). Similarly,
one's place in the hierarchy of being depends on the degree to
which one's *khudi* is developed: the earth's *khudi* is more powerful
than the moon's, and so the latter revolves around the former;
but the earth itself revolves around the sun since the sun's *khudi*
is more powerful than the earth's (AK, 15). Our main concern,
however, is human *khudi*, to which we now turn.

Iqbal does not define *khudi* in logically rigorous terms. Saying
only that *khudi* is a point of light, he equates *khudi* with life itself:
khudi is 'the spark of life in our dusty being' (AK, 18). But the
source of *khudi's* light is divine—'*Khudi* is lit up from the light
of the Majestic One'—and its very existence depends on Divine
existence (AHf, 1003). *Khudi* operates in, but does not belong to,
the physical world, and its time is not measured in terms of the
days and nights familiar to us (PM, 230). Compared with the rest
of creation, the human being possesses *khudi* in a relatively complete
form and, for this reason, tops the chain of created beings. But
while the independence of an individual human *khudi* is a positive
value, the isolation of one human *khudi* from another is not,
for such an isolation will cut off the members of a group from
one another; this allows each *khudi* to be a law unto itself, which,
potentially, could lead to a state of anarchy. Since individuals can
properly grow and develop only in interaction with one another,

it is necessary that the members of a society submit to a common code of conduct. Far from negating human freedom, submission to such a code channels it in wholesome ways, allowing each individual's *khudi* to reach its potential within a framework of harmony. For an Islamic society, such a code is the Sharia, which enjoins Muslims to believe in one God, obey the Prophet, and—following the Qur'an and the Prophet's normative practice—create a universal Muslim community that is free, egalitarian, and forward-looking. In this way, we progress from *khudi* to *bikhudi* or selflessness—that is, from *khudi* viewed in its individual capacity to *khudi* viewed in its social capacity. It would be correct to say that *khudi* reaches its full potential only when it becomes *bikhudi* (PM, 231; RB, 85–88).

Especially in *Asrar-i Khudi* (p. 18 ff.) and *Rumuz-i Bikhudi* (p. 85 ff.) but also in other works, Iqbal gives details of how *khudi* might be nurtured. He mentions factors that strengthen *khudi* (for example, love of God and the Prophet Muhammad, devotion to a noble cause, self-discipline, and struggle against odds) and factors that weaken it (for example, dependence on others and life-negating philosophy and literature). Iqbal equates *khudi* with life and both with action. It is through action—that is, through acceptance of life's challenges—that human *khudi* survives and becomes strong; inaction or inertia, on the other hand, spells its death. Life's hardships are not to be scorned or avoided: 'Hardships make *khudi* stronger' (JN, 638)—how delightful is the sight of a flowing stream hitting a rock and rolling around it! (AHf, 991). Nature poses a challenge to human *khudi*, which must set conquest of nature as its goal.

In developing his concept of *khudi*, Iqbal had a specific purpose in mind. At the start of the twentieth century, the majority of the world's Muslims were politically weak, economically backward, and socially disintegrated. To Iqbal, this general decadence of the Muslims was due to the fact that they had forgotten who they were, were ashamed to take pride in their glorious tradition, suffered from a crisis of self-confidence, lacked self-esteem, and had despaired of building a bright future for themselves—in a word, had allowed their *khudi* to waste away. The diagnosis suggested the cure, too: Muslims must rebuild their *khudi*, and they could do so by, above all, cultivating faith in their ability to find their own solutions to the problems facing them. Iqbal drives this point home by using a variety of images: Muslims should emulate not the moth, which circles alien light, but the glow-worm, which becomes its own lantern (PM, 287); they should not, when pitching a tent, borrow ropes from others (AHf, 944); they should remember the camel's advice to its colt: always carry your burden on your own back (AHf, 993); and they should, like the growing moon, draw their sustenance from their own being (AK, 23). Furthermore, instead of blaming God or fate for their misfortunes, Muslims must make an effort to change the world through their own efforts:

> It is futile to complain of Divine decree—
> Why are you yourself not Divine decree?
>
> (AHf, 998)

The survival of a nation, no less than that of individuals, depends on *khudi*. Accordingly, a nation, too, must guard and nurture its *khudi*. It can do so by honouring its tradition, for it is history that links up a nation's past, present, and future (RB, 145–8).

The concept of *khudi* furnishes Iqbal with a criterion of judgement: whatever nurtures *khudi* is good, and whatever kills or dampens *khudi* is bad. Thus, the philosophies that negate life, enervate society, and engender sloth are to be condemned, and the art and literature that divorce beauty from truth are decadent. Iqbal inveighs against Platonic thought: Plato, 'that old hermit' who 'fell victim to the magic spell of the insensible', 'denied the reality of the commotion of existence, creating, instead, invisible Forms' (AK, 32–3); Iqbal also calls him 'a sheep in man's clothing'—one who preferred dreaming to living and scorned action (AK, 33). For similar reasons Iqbal criticises the arts that have a soporific effect on people and kill their *khudi* instead of building it up (ZK, 562, 576, 580–1). Iqbal was of the opinion that the Arab element in the Islamic literary tradition was basically healthy, invigorating, and life-affirming, whereas the *'Ajami* or non-Arab element—especially that represented by some of the medieval Persian mystics—was effete and lethargy-inducing, and should, therefore, be avoided by Muslim readers. The man in whom *khudi* is fully developed is called the Perfect Man. The terms Iqbal uses to describe the Perfect Man include 'Man of Truth' (sometimes simply 'Man'), 'Free Man', and 'Believer' (one who is a true Muslim) or 'Believing Man'. The Perfect Man is not, like Nietzsche's Superman, a class unto himself and one who is beyond good and evil. Rather, he is the distillation of all that is best in humanity, the acme of human perfection—and, as such, the goal of all creation, the trophy that life strives to achieve. The Perfect Man does not sever links with the world of ordinary mortals—another contrast with Nietzsche's Superman—but rather sets them a model they may aspire after; he inspires and motivates them to rise to new levels of self-development. The Perfect Man 'infuses life into hearts' (*AHf*, 1018); he becomes the true representative of God on earth—Iqbal calls him *na'ib-i Haqq*, 'God's Vicegerent' (*AK*, 44). The Perfect Man directs the course of history, develops life's potentialities, and creates a society that is based on the principles of peace, equality, and justice (*AK*, 44–6). He embodies the wisdom of Gabriel and the Qur'an, delivers a revolutionary message to humankind, effects a radical transformation in people's lives, turning pieces of clay into shining pearls, and harnesses the forces of nature into his service (*PCBK*, 808–10). By aligning his will completely with God's will, the Perfect Man becomes Divine decree incarnate (*PCBK*, 809), his hand becoming the hand of God (*BJ*, 389). This world is waiting for the arrival of the Perfect Man (*AHf*, 935). More than that, God Himself is in search of such a man (*PM*, 210).

According to Iqbal, Muhammad is the Perfect Man. The Prophet's life-giving breath grew tulips in Arabia's desert, creating such outstanding personalities as Abu Bakr, 'Umar, 'Ali, and Husayn (*PCBK* 835; also *RB*, 95; *PM*, 188, 190). The Prophet, therefore, ought to command a Muslim's highest loyalty, for it is only by following him that one who is imperfect can hope to become perfect. In 'The Stream of Water' (*PM*, 299–300), which is a free translation of Goethe's poem 'Mahomets Gesang', Iqbal recounts how the stream (which stands for Muhammad), originating in the high mountains, travels down ecstatically into the plains—producing music as it strikes the rocks along the way and bringing spring in its wake—and, after incorporating many little streams in itself, becomes a huge flood that moves rapidly towards its final destination—the limitless ocean (which represents God). This poem can be read as describing the Perfect Man who, out of his concern and compassion for humanity, leads it on the path to perfection.

As can be seen, Iqbal's view of the Perfect Man—the highest embodiment of *khudi*—is neither apocalyptic nor messianic. The rise of the Perfect Man does not signify the end of history. The Perfect Man represents a model that is valid for all ages. Not only can there be more than one, ideally, there ought to be many more than one Perfect Man at a given time. Nor does the Perfect Man render all value-scales obsolete or irrelevant. On the contrary, he represents a realization of the fullest moral potential that human beings are capable of realizing. Iqbal's designation of Muhammad as the Perfect Man is to be interpreted in the context of the oft-stressed fact of Muhammad's humanity. Thus, in emulating Muhammad, one is only trying to reach a level of perfection that both befits one as a moral being and is very much within human reach. The concept of the Perfect Man is best understood as a philosophico-poetic representation of the familiar religious idea of Muhammad as the worthiest of human models, such that the concept is never devoid of legal and moral content.

IV. LIFE AS QUEST

The theme of *khudi* is closely linked in Iqbal with that of life as quest and discovery. In 'Conquest of Nature', Adam, on coming out of paradise, says that he is a 'martyr to quest' (PM, 257). We have already noted that Iqbal is critical of philosophies that accord preference to supine contemplation over vigorous action. The mandate of humans is to bring out their potential to the fullest and to change and mould the world after their hearts' desire.

The two missions are related since conquest of nature is an important way in which human beings affirm their *khudi*. The following passage from *Asrar-i Khudi* forcefully states Iqbal's philosophy of action (the reference in line 4 is to Qur'an 21. 68–71, which relates how God rescued Abraham when he was thrown into a fire by the king of his time):

> Action sums up the lesson of life;
> The joy of creation is the law of life.
> Rise, and be a creator of a new world;
> With flames about you, earn the fame of Abraham.
> To conform to a contrary world
> Is to lay down arms on the battlefield.
> The world itself conforms to the ways
> Of a self-respecting, seasoned man.
> And if the world does not conform to his ways,
> He declares war against the heavens.
> He destroys the foundations of the existing world,
> And gives a new formation to the atoms.
> He disrupts the revolution of days and nights,
> And turns the blue sky upside down.
> By his own power he brings into being
> A new world that is friendlier to him.
> If it is not possible to live like men in the world,
> Then to lay down one's life like men—that is life!
>
> (AK, 49)

Since the human potential is limitless and the task of conquering nature never-ending, life becomes a series of quests. We must progress from one stage to another, never resting on our laurels, always regarding our destination only as another milestone along the way (PM, 215).

Success in life requires strength, and one becomes strong not by passively conforming to the given scheme of things, but by putting the stamp of one's personality on the resistant environment: the same substance becomes coal through passive conformity to the environment, but it becomes a shining diamond when it seeks to assert itself by challenging the environment (AK,

56–7). The same is true of the ant, which was condemned to be an ant because it chose to search for its food in the dust, as opposed to the eagle, which thinks little of the nine heavens (BJ, 461). A keen student of human history, Iqbal was convinced that, for a nation, to be weak is to be vulnerable—in one place, he calls weakness a sin whose wages is death (BJ, 449)—and that a nation can live a life of dignity only if it has power: 'It is strength that makes a life of honour possible' (AK, 57). But Iqbal does not glorify power for its own sake. Might must be informed by right: 'Power and truth are twins' (AK, 50). It is on this principled understanding of the relationship of might and right that Iqbal criticises, on the one hand, the unscrupulous conduct of European powers in the international arena and, on the other hand, the apologetic and obsequious attitude of those Muslim leaders and scholars who, eager to prove Islam's pacifism, would not allow Muslim nations to fight even in the face of blatant aggression.

Power is not the only quality Iqbal admires. He leaves plenty of room in life for the play of the finer human feelings. His ideal is a man who has a body of steel that houses a tender, compassionate heart. The following is one of Iqbal's finest quatrains:

> Build, with your handful of dust,
> A body stronger than a rock fortress,
> And inside this body let there be a heart that feels sorrow—
> Like a stream flowing by a mountain.

> (PM, 199)

The importance of action in life derives from the very nature of existence. Heraclitus taught that everything is in a state of constant flux. Even though Iqbal believed in the existence of certain absolute or permanent moral values that ought to guide and inspire human beings, the Heraclitean insight, Iqbal would seem to think, is valuable for the purpose, first, of intelligently and effectively translating those moral values into action in real-life situations, and, second, of making the evolution of the human spirit or mind possible. 'Change', Iqbal accordingly remarks, 'is the only constant in the world' (BD 148). Properly mediated change brings strength:

The cup of life gains strength through perpetual motion;
This, ignorant one, is the secret of life's eternity.

(BD, 258)

True change, in Iqbal's view, originates in the deepest recesses
of the human self, from where it springs forth like the water
of a fountain, so to speak, and manifests itself in the world outside.
Human beings can transform society only if their own spirits
undergo transformation first. On this subject, one can do no
better than to quote from Iqbal's Introduction to *Payam-i Mashriq*:

The East, especially the Islamic East, has reawakened after a continuous
slumber that lasted for centuries. But the nations of the East should
realize that life cannot bring about a revolution in its external environment
until change first occurs in its own inmost depths, and that no new
world can appear in the external world until its existence is first mapped
out in people's hearts and minds. This ineluctable law of nature, which
the Qur'an [13. 11] has expressed in its simple but eloquent words—
'God does not change a people's condition until the people change
their own condition'—encompasses both the individual and the collective
aspects of life, and it is this truth that I have tried to keep in view
in my Persian writings. (PM, 182)

V. INTELLECT AND LOVE

A major theme in Iqbal's poetry is that of *'aql* and *'ishq* and their
relationship. *'Aql* is reason, or rather discursive or analytic reason;
Iqbal uses *khirad* as a synonym for it. *'Ishq*, literally passionate
love, represents a group of ideas: intuition, which, unlike *'aql*,
grasps reality in a swift, synthetic sweep; deep and selfless devotion
to an ideal, or earnestness of purpose; and vigorous and dynamic
action, which guarantees success in the battlefield of life. These
meanings of *'ishq* are integrally related to one another, though
one of them may predominate in a given context. Here we will
use the words Intellect and Love to denote *'aql* and *'ishq*, respectively.
(The capitalization of the two English terms not only underscores
their importance, but also reflects the fact that Iqbal frequently
personifies *'aql* and *'ishq*.)

Intellect deals with the sensible world. It serves an important function in that it guides us through the maze of life by providing answers to problems that are amenable to logical analysis. Since it operates on the physical world and in historical time, it has certain in-built limitations: 'Intellect is a prisoner of today and tomorrow [serial time]; it is a worshipper of the idols that can be seen or heard' (PM, 209). It can witness only a slice of reality at one point of time—it is given to 'worshipping of the part' (AK, 13)—and that is why the sages have failed to explain fully the truth about the human being, not to speak of the truth about the angels or God (PM, 234). Quite understandably—and deservedly, one might add—Intellect lacks certitude (AHf, 1019). Being unsure of itself, it is always busy weighing up the pros and cons of a matter and, worrying as it does over the possible consequences of an action, drags its feet in a situation that calls for bold action. Not so Love, which resides in the heart and, like the heart, is free from the limitations of time. Unlike Intellect, Love has no vested interests to guard and no ulterior motives to camouflage. And so, unlike Intellect, which—embodying itself in hypocritical religious persons and clever but none-too-moral individuals— becomes crafty and devious, Love remains simple and altruistic. It unhesitatingly takes the plunge when called upon to act: 'Love emboldens the pheasants to take on eagles' (PM, 196). Alluding to the idolatrous king Nimrod's attempt to burn Abraham the monotheist in a fire, Iqbal cites Abraham as the paradigm of Love:

> Love jumped fearlessly into Nimrod's fire—
> Intellect, on the rooftop, is still absorbed in the view below.
>
> (BD, 278)

Love is by far more resourceful than Intellect. The secrets of life are revealed not through book-reading but through active engagement with the realities of existence. In a short poem, 'Book-Worm', the insect (representing Intellect) complains that its long perusal of books has not revealed to it the wisdom of life, to which a moth—the self-immolating devotee of burning light—

responds that fervent and committed action alone lays bare the mysteries of life (PM, 273–4).

Notwithstanding the differences between them (several passages in Iqbal's poems—for example, RB, 109–11—offer a sustained contrast between the two), Intellect and Love have a deep mutual affinity. In fact, they are united in essence, purpose, and function. Both are born of *arzu*—the 'desire' to seek and discover (AK, 16)—both thus being goal-directed (ZA, 412). Intellect, while it lacks the freedom and range of Love, is by no means without merit. Indispensable as an organizing principle of life, it is needed, along with Love, for the purpose of improving the quality of life. The heart, which is Love's residence, must, therefore, be lit up by the light of Intellect, and the judgements of Intellect must, similarly, be evaluated at the bar of Love (PM, 241). Ideally, then, Intellect and Love should complement and reinforce each other in the interest of making harmonious life possible. Iqbal's poem 'A Dialogue between Knowledge and Love' (in Iqbal, knowledge often appears as an ally of Intellect, and so can be taken as representing Intellect in this poem) can be seen as stating Iqbal's final position on the matter. In this poem, after an exchange between Knowledge and Love, in which each argues for its superiority over the other, Love settles the argument in the following words:

> Come—turn this earthly world into a garden,
> And make the old world young again.
> Come—take just a little of my heart's solicitude,
> And build, under the heavens, an everlasting paradise.
> We have been on intimate terms since the day of creation,
> And are the high and low notes of the same song.
>
> (PM, 268)

VI. ISLAM AS A LIVING FAITH

Islam—both as religion and as civilization—is central to Iqbal's thought and poetry. Iqbal stood for Islam as a living faith. While some of his prose writings offer a keen philosophical treatment of Islamic doctrine, he is unlike a typical Muslim theologian in that his main focus, especially in his poetry, is Islam as a lived reality.

Iqbal was critically appreciative of early Islamic history. He firmly believed in the validity of the Islamic Project initiated by Muhammad in seventh-century Arabia. Guided by Divine revelation, the Prophet aimed at establishing a model community that would at once be religious and humane, spiritual and egalitarian. But, in Iqbal's view, while the Islamic Project under Muhammad and his immediate successors did produce the desired results, it later went off course, with disastrous results—even though, from time to time and here and there, the project was revived in part, leading Muslims to make remarkable achievements in diverse areas. The stagnation and decadence of the worldwide Muslim community thus became a main preoccupation of the poet Iqbal.

Analysing the decay of the Muslim community, Iqbal points to the failure of the Muslim leaders, Muslim masses, and Muslim institutions. Some of his sharpest criticism is aimed at the religious scholars and spiritual guides—the Mullas and the Sufis. The Mullas are given to petty in-fighting, and they have made mosques, which are houses of worship, into their fiefs: 'Two Mullas cannot live in one mosque' (AHf, 979). The seminary run by the Mulla is, on account of its outdated curriculum and dull atmosphere, like a sandy desert that lacks the redeeming feature of a water fountain (AHf, 930). The Mulla claims to be a Muslim, but his questionable way of practising Islam alienates people from Islam—it even turns Muslims into nonbelievers (JN, 664). The Sufi in his monastery was supposed to establish a close and personal relationship with God, but his interests have shifted from single-minded remembrance of God to preoccupation with stories and legends (ZA, 415). The spiritual wine, once his proud possession, no longer intoxicates him with love of God, but rather has become an excuse for lethargy and inaction (ZK, 500). Both the Mulla and the Sufi have failed to carry on the Prophetic mission of disseminating authentic knowledge of Islam and serving as role models of piety and learning. They are only too willing to serve the ruling classes (AHu, 648),

and inexcusable ignorance and mundane motives have caused
them to misinterpret the scriptures and mislead ordinary Muslims:

> My greetings to the Mulla and the Sufi,
> For they delivered God's message to us!
> But their interpretation of it has left
> God, Gabriel, and Muhammad astonished.
>
> (AHf, 956)

The religious leaders of the community are not the only ones
to blame. The intellectual leaders fare no better. The Muslim
philosophers have written authoritative disquisitions on matters
of which they have no sure knowledge; they are like an author
who writes a book on pearl-diving without ever having dived into
the sea (AHf, 994). The theologian is interested in investigating
the sterile issues of whether the attributes of God are identical
with or distinct from God's being and whether the Qur'an, the
speech of God, is co-eternal with God or came into existence
at a later time (AHu, 656). Then there is the Westernized Muslim
who criticizes the men of religion for neglecting their responsibilities,
forgetting that he himself is no worthier representative of Islam:

> Iqbal said to the shaykh of the Ka'bah
> 'Who fell sleep under the very arch in the mosque?'
> A voice sounded from the walls of the mosque:
> 'Who became lost in the idol-house of the West?'
>
> (AHu, 673)

Both the religiously-minded and the secularly-oriented suffer from
the malaise known as taqlid, uncritical acceptance of authority:
the former can do no better than to follow blindly the old schools
of law; the latter only know how to imitate the West. (Iqbal
was suspicious of Turkey's secularism, fearing that, in breaking
with their Islamic past, the Turks were only putting on the yoke
of the West (JN, 950, 974).) Both the religious and the secular
groups lack the spirit of independent inquiry and, consequently,
are incapable of meeting the ever-new challenges presented
by life.

As for the common people, their lives are marked by schism and lack of purpose, and their attachment to Islam is mostly sentimental:

> Muslims are at war with one another—
> And in their hearts they harbour only schism;
> They cry out if someone pulls out a brick
> From the mosque which they themselves shun.

(AHf, 921)

The historic Muslim institutions which once bristled with life and effectively met the real needs of society have now become barren or moribund. The fate that befell the Mulla's school and the Sufi's monastery also befell the political system, which degenerated from caliphate—which upheld the justice-based Sharia—to kingship—whose hallmarks are cunning and deception (AHf, 972). All in all, today's Muslim is a far cry from his former self. He possesses neither military nor financial power, and his connection with the nourishing roots of his tradition, which is centred round the Book of God, is all but severed:

> His pure blood has lost its brilliance,
> And tulips no longer grow in his wasteland.
> His scabbard is empty, just like his purse,
> And his Book is in the vault of a house in ruins.

(AHf, 914)

The principal physical symbol of Islam is the Ka'bah, which Abraham had built in Makka and consecrated to the worship of the One God. Muhammad purged it of the idols that polytheists had later placed in it, and rededicated it to monotheistic worship. But while the Ka'bah today is free of graven images and wooden statues, it has come to house, thanks to the Muslims' ignorance and neglect, idols of a different kind—idols of schism and bigotry, hypocrisy and complacence, and formalism and ritualism:

> The Ka'bah is populated by our idols—
> Disbelief laughs at our belief!

(AK, 70)

In a word, the Muslim is no longer worthy of his name. He suffers from a lack of what Iqbal calls *khudi* or selfhood (see Section III, above). Outwardly, he seem to be fine—his bodily frame is sturdy—'but the wise physician knows from the look in his eyes, that his *khudi* is paralysed within him' (*AHf*, 918).

The situation is not entirely hopeless, though. Just as Muhammad was the final prophet, raised by God to guide humankind, so the Muslims are the final community (*RB*, 102; in *RB*, 81, Iqbal coins the phrase *khatam-i aqwam*, the 'seal of the nations', on the analogy of Qur'an 33. 40, where Muhammad is called *khatam al-nabiyyin*, the 'seal of the prophets') raised by God to establish truth and justice in the world. The Muslim community is not without signs of life—'the old bough still has some moisture left in it' (*AHf*, 964), and 'this wine-cup still has a few drops of drink left in it' (*PM*, 223). The Muslim, after all, believes in God and possesses some of His attributes (*AHf*, 965). Moreover, it was from Muslim civilization that the modern West drew its inspiration, and many of the furnishings and appurtenances that adorn the West's mansion have been borrowed from Muslims (*AK*, 74). All this suggests that the Muslims are capable of creating a new world and ushering in a new era. Armed with this hope and confidence, Iqbal offers a programme for the renewal of the worldwide Muslim community.

Muslims must begin by renewing their commitment to their religion. They must drink the same 'old wine' (*AHf*, 989), again pledging, like their early ancestors (*PM*, 190, 191), to emulate the Prophet in their lives (*RB*, 81). They must hold fast to their primary source of inspiration and insight, the Qur'an. If they truly act upon the Qur'an, they can, like their illustrious forebears, bring about earth-shaking changes in the world (*AHf*, 955). In several sections of *Rumuz-i Bikhudi* (91–155), Iqbal states and explains in detail what he calls the basic pillars of the Islamic community. Monotheism, of course, tops the list. Belief in one God is the source of all good, all insight, and all power; it provides a focal point for thought, feeling, and action; it gives hope and courage, cutting off fear and despair; and it establishes equality among Muslims while setting them free from all types of bondage. Next comes prophecy. It was the Prophet Muhammad who conveyed the message of God to Muslims and elucidated it for them; who established, in practice, an egalitarian system of law and ethics; and who knit Muslims into a unified community—unified not on the basis of the narrow principle of territorial nationalism but on the basis of the belief that the creatures of one God make one humanity. Muhammad brought with him the Qur'an, Islam's foundational text, and this book must serve as the eternal source of guidance for Muslims, constituting the core of the Islamic code of conduct known as the Sharia. The Ka'bah, where Muslims coming from all over the world perform the pilgrimage, serves as the visible or tangible centre of Muslim unity.

But commitment to Islam will not by itself work miracles. Muslims must realize that 'life is struggle and not a set of rights' to be claimed unconditionally (PM, 190). They should understand that the particular community to which they belong requires them to sink their tribal, ethnic, cultural, racial, and linguistic differences so that they might create a body politic that is founded on Islam's universal and inclusive principles; a Muslim's first identity is as a Muslim, not as an Afghan, Turk, or Tartar (PM, 222). They must also learn the lesson of self-reliance: they should be like the self-respecting Turkish sailor who sang as he rowed his boat, saying that if he ran into trouble on the high seas, he would call upon none other than the storm itself for help (PM, 962).

At the heart both of Iqbal's critique of the Muslim community and of his programme for the community's rejuvenation is the insight that Islam is an active and living principle, that Muslims in their early history were able to turn Islam into a world religion and a world civilization on the entirely valid assumption that life calls upon one to act—with foresight and courage—and that sterile speculation and hollow formalism in a community are sure signs of decay and death. In one of his best-known poems, 'Iblis's Advisory Council', Iblis, or Satan, tells his advisors what they must do in order to perpetuate the Muslims' abject state. Make sure, he says, that they remain busy spinning cobwebs of speculation and splitting hairs over niggling details of religion, so that they might lose touch with the real world, where success and progress depend on taking wise and daring action (AHu, 656–7).

VII. THE PROPHET AND THE QUR'AN

Muslims revere Muhammad not only as one who conveyed to them the Divine revelation called the Qur'an, but also as one who was a living embodiment of the Qur'an, offering his followers a perfect model for emulation. Muslim veneration for the Prophet is expressed at the popular as well as at the intellectual level, and a whole genre of Prophet's eulogy has come into existence in several languages. Iqbal's poems in praise of the Prophet are among the gems of Persian and Urdu literature. The following lines will give an idea of Iqbal's deep devotion to the Prophet:

> He—the one who knew the ways of truth,
> Was the seal of the prophets,
> And was the lord of all—
> The one who endowed the pathway's dust
> With the brilliant light of the Valley of Sinai.
> In the eyes of love and ecstasy he is the First and the Last—
> He is the Qur'an, and he the Criterion,
> He is the Ya-Sin, and he the Ta-Ha!

> (BJ, 317)

(In the last three lines, the phrase 'the First and the Last' is taken from Qur'an 57. 3, where God is so described; 'Ya-Sin' and 'Ta-Ha' are the names of two Qur'anic suras, thirty-sixth and twentieth, respectively; and 'Criterion' is one of the names of the Qur'an (25. 1).)

Muhammad, according to Iqbal, is the focal point of the ideal Muslim polity. In his poem 'Nationalism' (BD, 160–1), Iqbal attacks territorial nationalism because it is opposed to the religion taught by Muhammad. If one had to choose a geographical place to 'localize' the Muslim community, it would not be India, Persia, or Syria; it would be Yathrib—the pre-Islamic name of Madina, the Prophet's city: 'Ah, Yathrib, you are the Muslim's country and his refuge' (BD, 147). Muhammad, the 'chief' of the Hijaz in Arabia, is 'the leader of our caravan' (BD, 159), and 'Islam is your country, you are a follower of the Chosen Prophet' (BD, 147). In 'Iblis's Advisory Council', Iblis tells his advisors that they can perpetuate Satanic rule in the world by making sure that Muslims will remain ignorant of Muhammad's code of conduct, which brings out the best in men by putting them to the test, protects women's honour, abolishes slavery of all kinds, establishes equality among all human beings, and teaches the affluent to use their wealth responsibly (AHf, 654–5). It was Muhammad who demonstrated, through his conduct, how to create a synthesis of the religious and the worldly, or the spiritual and the mundane: 'He unlocked the gates of the world by means of the key of religion' (AK, 19). In Jawid-Namah, in the section entitled 'Tasin-i Muhammad' (pp. 642–3), the spirit of Abu Jahl, one of Muhammad's staunchest opponents, visits the Ka'bah, once an idol-house, lamenting that Muhammad has worked havoc with Arabia's religion and tradition by introducing a monotheistic and egalitarian system. In several sections of Rumuz-i Bikhudi (pp. 100–40), Iqbal explains the mission of the Prophet.

In Iqbal's view, then, Muhammad deserves praise and respect not only because he is the bearer and exemplifier of the Divine message, but also because he is, for Muslims, the most potent source of inspiration and the most important reference point for action. Muslims must love the Prophet with all their hearts and souls, so that their love of him becomes the driving force in their lives, enabling them to reach perfection. Since it was through Muhammad, a man of flesh and blood like them, that they received Divine guidance, Muslims are justified in saying that, in a sense, 'The Prophet becomes even dearer than God' (RB, 101), and that while 'You can deny God, you cannot deny the glory of Muhammad' (PM, 353). And they may also say that, in a sense, Madina, the city which the Prophet chose for his residence and where he is buried, is dearer to them than Makka, the city where the Ka'bah, the House of God, is located. Addressing God, Iqbal says:

My body is weary, but my soul moves briskly
To the city in whose path lies Makka.
You stay here and mix with the elite,
For it is my friend's city I wish to reach.

(*AHf*, 901)

And addressing Muhammad, he says:

It was at your command that we set out for Makka,
Otherwise our destination is none but you.

(*AHf*, 928)

Iqbal once remarked that non-Muslims may not be able to appreciate
fully the depth of the Muslims' fondness for their prophet. Be
that as it may, Iqbal's poetry illustrates, for both Muslims and
non-Muslims, how love of Muhammad can inspire one of the most
distinguished Muslim thinkers of modern times.

Iqbal claims that his poetry revolves around the Qur'an, and
says that if his verses have any non-Qur'anic content, then he may
not have, on Judgement Day, the privilege of kissing the Prophet's
feet (*RB*, 168). The statement shows Iqbal's understanding of
his role as a poet: he would use his poetry to expound the Qur'an.
And to be sure, there is plenty of evidence of the Qur'an-centredness
of Iqbal's poetry. To begin with, Iqbal's verses contain countless
citations from the Qur'an. In many cases, individual words or
short phrases—sometimes complete sentences—are cited verbatim.
Qur'an 2. 138 instructs Muslims to be 'dyed' in the colour of God;
it opens with the phrase *Sibghata llah*, 'Take on the hue of God',
which is seamlessly incorporated in Iqbal's line, *Qalb ra az sibghata
llah rang dih* (*AK*, 62), 'Dye your heart in God's colour'. Qur'an
3. 92 encourages Muslims to make monetary sacrifice in the way
of God. The opening part, *Lan tanalu l-birra hatta tunfiqu*, 'You
will never attain to piety until you spend [of that which you love]'
forms a complete hemistich in one of Iqbal's couplets (*JN*, 668).
A number of Persian and Urdu verses contain exact or near-
exact renderings or interpretations of Qur'anic verses. For example,
Ma zi ni'mat'ha-i u ikhwan shudem, 'It was by His mercy that we

became brothers' is a translation of Qur'an 3. 103, *Fa-asbahtum bi-ni'mati llahi ikhwanan*, 'And so you became brothers, by God's blessing'. Sometimes Iqbal adapts Qur'anic words or expressions, slightly modifying the wording or structure, to suit metrical or other needs.

The innumerable citations from the Qur'an in Iqbal's poetry show the Qur'an's influence on Iqbal's diction. But the influence runs much deeper. To Iqbal, the Qur'an not only represents the ultimate authority in Islam, but also contains the guidance needed for making a Muslim renaissance possible. In *Jawid-Namah*, Sa'id Halim Pasha (d. 1917), Muslim reformer and Turkey's grand vizier, invites Muslims to turn to the Qur'an and receive direction from it: 'Embedded in its verses', he says, 'are a hundred new worlds', and he adds that the Qur'an will help Muslims replace the old world with a new one (*JN*, 654). In the same work, another modern Muslim reformer, Jamal al-Din al-Afghani, gives details of the four foundational concepts (*muhkamat*) of the 'Qur'anic world' (*JN*, 656–63): the vicegerency of Adam, Divine rule, Divine ownership of the earth, and wisdom as a great good. In the interest of brevity, it need only be noted that all these concepts, even the words in which they are couched, are derived from the Qur'an, representing Iqbal's conviction that a programme of revitalization of the Muslim community must be based on the Qur'an.

Most intriguing, perhaps, is Iqbal's interpretation of Qur'anic thought. This subject, as indeed the entire subject of Iqbal's use of the Qur'an in his works, requires detailed study. Here we will make only a few remarks. Iqbal planned to write a commentary on the Qur'an. He did not live to execute that plan, but his works, especially his poetry, give us a glimpse of the lines along which such a work might have proceeded. It seems that Iqbal's concern was not to produce a work along traditional lines—a verse-by-verse commentary on the grammar, theology, and law of the Qur'an—but to write a work that would bring out the dynamic nature of the Islamic Scripture, highlighting, especially, the applied aspects of lessons learnt from the Qur'an. A fine example of this approach is found in the concluding sections of *Rumuz-i Bikhudi*, where Iqbal summarizes the contents of the book by offering a commentary on the 112th sura of the Qur'an (*RB*, 156–65). This sura, called *Ikhlas* (Sincerity), consists of only four verses:

> Say: He—God—is Uniquely One;
> God is the Independent One;
> He did not beget, and He was not begotten;
> And none is a peer unto Him.

Iqbal comments that, like God, who is one (verse 1), Muslims must become a single, unified community; that, like God, who does not depend on any other being for His subsistence (verse 2), Muslims must become self-reliant, drawing out their own potential instead of living on the kindness of others; that, like God, who neither begets nor was begotten (verse 3), Muslims must reject lineage as the basis of their identity—since their primary and real identity is religious and not tribal or ethnic; and that, like God, who is peerless (verse 4), Muslims must become peerless among the nations of the world. These sections of *Rumuz-i Bikhudi* contain some memorable lines, whose power, unfortunately, is much diminished in translation: 'Be one, giving visible form to monotheism' (p. 157); 'How long will you [moth-like] circle the lamp of the assembly? If you possess a heart, burn yourself with your own fire' (p. 161); 'The bond of love [of God] is stronger than the bond of lineage' (p. 163); and 'You must strengthen your bonds with "He who is peerless" so that you, too, become unique among the nations' (p. 164).

With the possible exception of Rumi and a few others, no other Muslim poet has grounded his poetry in the Qur'an in a manner similar to Iqbal's.

VIII. EAST AND WEST

By 'West', Iqbal usually means the modern Western world— especially Europe—and its civilization, but sometimes he means by it one or more countries of colonial Europe, such as England, France, and Italy. By 'East', he means Asia and its civilizations—

especially the Indian subcontinent and the Islamic world, though frequently he means by it the Islamic world only. Iqbal often mentions the East and West together in a context of contrast, sometimes praising one at the expense of the other, but sometimes criticizing both. The contemplative East is lost in the world of spirit and has a negative attitude towards life and matter, failing to make an effective response to changes that occur in real life and to achieve material success. The action-oriented West, on the other hand, is alive to the needs of change and adapts itself to the changing material circumstances. But its disregard of the call of the spirit has stunted its spiritual growth. Thus, both the East and the West fail on serious counts, the former lacking dynamism, the latter lacking depth:

> I have seen many a tavern of the East and of the West:
> Here the cup-bearer is missing, there the wine is insipid.

> (BD, 315)

The servile East continues to follow antiquated ways of thought and action—it is still worshipping old idols; the West has smashed the old idols, only to replace them with new ones. In *Jawid-Namah*, Iqbal makes the Buddha say:

> Be it Western wisdom or Eastern philosophy,
> Both are idol-houses—and it is pointless to circle idols.

> (JN, 634)

While Iqbal is severely critical of both the East and the West, his criticism of the West is more unsparing: 'The East is in bad shape, the West is worse' (ZA, 42). Iqbal is philosophically opposed to some of the major assumptions underlying modern Western culture. He disapproves of the divorce of politics from religion and ethics, for the divorce has, in his view, deprived the West of a sound source of knowledge and inspiration: 'Divorced from politics, religion is reduced to Chenghizship' (BJ, 332). In the long poem 'Guide along the Path', Iqbal offers a scathing criticism of the nationalistic and racist doctrines of the West, and also of

the collusion of Christianity with the dominant, but unscrupulous,
Western powers:

Race, nationalism, church, kingdom, civilization, colour—
What choice intoxicants Mastership has created!

(BD, 262)

In the same poem, Iqbal remarks that Western democracy is only
disguised Caesarship and that Western legislatures are controlled
by capitalists (BD, 261). Capitalism and communism are two
millstones between which humanity is being crushed (JN, 653).
The international conduct of Europe's so-called democracies is
as unconscionable as that of Italy's fascism. In a poem, Mussolini,
when taken to task by his fellow European rulers for his imperialism,
retorts that their own record in this regard is hardly better (ZK,
611–2). Iqbal also criticizes the West for breaking up the unity
of the Muslim world and for dealing with Muslims in an unfair
and high-handed manner in the wake of World War I (BD, 264).

Iqbal was critical of Western learning, which, according to him,
is based strictly on sense perception and denies the validity of
knowledge obtained through other avenues:

Modern learning is the greatest barrier—
Idol-worshipper, idol-seller, idol-maker!
Its feet are tied to the prison of the sensibles;
It has never jumped across the sensory limits.

(AK, 68)

Western knowledge, while it dazzles with its intellectual brilliance,
lacks the immediacy and warmth of spirit:

Do not take offence, just give it a try:
The West enlightens the mind but spells ruin to the heart.

(BJ, 335)

And Iqbal was convinced that Western civilization's inherent
contradictions jeopardized its survival. The following lines are
from a poem he wrote during his stay in England:

> Your civilization will use its own dagger to take its life;
> The nest built on a delicate branch cannot last.

(BD, 141)

To some extent, Iqbal's criticism of the West is motivated by practical considerations. After the debacle of 1857, when the British formally occupied India, removing Muslims from seats of power, the majority of India's Muslims turned inward, viewing a passive guarding of their religion-based tradition as their prime duty and shunning contact with the dominant European culture. This large group felt that the West had nothing positive or useful to offer to Muslims. Another group of Muslims, which was at first small but grew in strength and number as time passed, took Europe as its ideal and sought to become Westernized—a slavish attitude that, according to Iqbal, was born of an inferiority complex. To both these groups, Iqbal emphasized the need to sift what was valuable in the West from what was worthless. He gave his own example: he had gone to Europe in search of knowledge and returned enriched—without allowing himself to be 'trapped' by the West (the last line in the following quatrain alludes to the Nimrod-Abraham incident already cited above):

> I broke the spell of modern learning:
> I took away the bait and broke the trap.
> God knows with what indifference,
> Like Abraham, I sat in its fire!

(Ahf, 934)

But in spite of his bitter criticism of the West, Iqbal was deeply appreciative of many of its aspects. He himself had drunk deep at the Western founts of scholarship, and he spoke with nostalgia about his stay in Europe. Both in his prose and in his poetry, he gives generous praise to distinguished Western figures—Sir Thomas Arnold, his teacher in Lahore and his mentor during his stay in Europe, being only one of those admired personalities. Iqbal believed that the West had once learnt from the Muslim world and that now it was the Muslims' turn to learn from the

West. Much of Iqbal's influence on the Muslims of India and other countries derives from his ability to draw creatively on Western as well as Eastern traditions of learning.

IX. CONCLUDING NOTE

Iqbal was conscious of his distinction as a poet. A verse in *Zabur-i 'Ajam* reads:

> A dove, singer of old songs, heard my lament and said,
> 'No one ever sang in the garden yesteryear's song in a strain like this.'

> (ZA, 410)

The thematic diversity of Iqbal's poetry alone will ensure Iqbal a place of honour in the history of Urdu and Persian poetry—in fact, in the history of the Islamic poetical tradition as such. One might even say that Iqbal's use of the poetical medium finds few parallels in the world's literary tradition. He uses poetry not only to express feelings, but also to discuss metaphysical, political, and economic issues, to comment on cultural and artistic matters, to reflect on the human existential situation, and—above all—to contribute to the transformation of individual and collective life in accordance with the dictates of an all-embracing ethical vision. As learned and astute a critic as Aziz Ahmad has remarked that the only other poets whose work could be compared with Iqbal's in respect of its synthesis of world thought are Dante in the Middle Ages and Goethe in modern times. 'To my knowledge', says Aziz Ahmad, 'there is no other poet who has exercised such deep and enduring influence on his nation's future' (*Na'i Tashkil*, p. 7).

3

Poetic Art

'Matthew Arnold defines poetry as criticism of life. That life is criticism of poetry is equally true' (SR, 49). These words of Iqbal sum up both his credo of poetry and his practice of poetry. Rejecting the idea of art for art's sake, Iqbal used poetry to state and argue for a carefully formed and passionately held world-view. But, although Iqbal is a poet with a message, his poetry cannot be called didactic or moralistic in a narrow sense. His art serves his thought without becoming its hostage, and always retains independent merit *qua* art. The remarkable union or synthesis of art and thought in Iqbal accounts for his pre-eminence as a poet. It also represents a level of achievement no other poet in the Indian subcontinent—or in the Persian-speaking world—after him has been able to match. Fortunately or unfortunately, one cannot speak of an Iqbalian poetical tradition.

Be that as it may, the hallmark of Iqbal's poetry is a very high degree of consonance between that poetry's substance and form. Our treatment of the art of Iqbal's poetry, like our treatment of the themes of his poetry, is going to be selective. We will look at some of the more general features of his poetry, without examining, for example, his—highly discriminating—use of different sub-genres of poetry or different metres for different purposes or occasions. Also, some of the features of Iqbal's poetry can be fully appreciated only in the original Persian and Urdu languages, such as internal rhyme, juxtaposition of semantically balanced expressions, use of words with a euphonic or musical quality, and certain forms of paronomasia.

I. DICTION

Iqbal, whose native tongue was Punjabi, had made a deep study of Urdu, Persian, and Arabic languages and literature. His mastery of the literary traditions of these languages is reflected in his diction. Iqbal wrote his first poems in Urdu, and they include a few poems for children written in very simple language. As a rule, however, Iqbal writes in what may be called High Urdu and High Persian, his poetry acquiring early on its distinctive quality, which is best described by the Arabic word *jalal* or the Persian word *shikoh*, both signifying 'majesty, stateliness, grandeur'. Iqbal's adoption of Persian as the vehicle of his mature thought added to that *jalal* or *shikoh*, since he was now able to draw freely on the vast reservoir of a language developed and refined over centuries by a long line of Persian masters. Iqbal's Persian is heavily influenced by Arabic literary models: Persian poets like Rumi, Sa'di, and Hafiz frequently and effortlessly weave Arabic phrases and sentences into their verse. Iqbal's own study of Arabic reinforces the Arabic 'effect' of his poetry. Generally speaking, therefore, Iqbal's language is rather difficult for an average reader of Urdu or Persian to follow. It is no surprise that, in the Indian subcontinent especially, the decline of Arabic and Persian learning has resulted in fewer and fewer people being able to appreciate the larger body of Iqbal's poetry.

What we have called the *jalal* or *shikoh* of Iqbal's poetry results, one might think, from his use of high-sounding words and expressions. That, however, is not the case. Iqbal's vocabulary is, ultimately, instrumental in character; he uses it to convey his understanding of life and reality. He holds, for example, that existence is marked by perpetual change and movement. To begin with, the cosmos is in motion—the stars, the moon, and the sun are all travelling through space. But Iqbal does not simply note

the fact of change and movement; he sees meaning in the fact:
the heavenly bodies are in motion because they are earnestly
pursuing a goal or seeking a destination. Noting a similar change
and movement in human history, in human society, and in the
individual human being, Iqbal seeks correspondences between
the condition of human beings and the condition of the heavenly
bodies. He goes one step further. Not content to situate the human
being within the cosmos, he seeks to incorporate and telescope
the cosmos within the human being: the human being is the
primary fact—the Adam created by God and meant to rule over
the universe—all other existence enjoying only secondary status;
it is the human being who manages and exploits the world and
assigns value to it. In principle, then, the human being towers
above the universe, the story of the human being thus becoming
the story of a being with a stature and importance next only
to God's—a being whom Iqbal calls God's colleague (PM, 198).

Given this epic-like setting of his poetry, Iqbal's diction acquires
a power that is as authentic as it is natural. To continue with
the motif of movement, Iqbal seems to be at his best when he
is describing movement, whether physical or metaphorical. The
following few lines describe the joyous movement of the mountain
stream in 'Ode to the Cup-Bearer':

> The mountain stream over there—it bounds,
> It halts, it curves, it glides,
> It leaps, it slides, it gathers itself,
> After much winding and turning, it sallies forth.

(BJ, 415)

The following Persian couplet, which is made up of ten verbs—
five in each hemistich—paints a vivid picture of the multifarious
activity of khudi:

> Khezad, angezad, parad, tabad, ramad,
> Sozad, afrozad, kushad, mirad, damad.
> It rises, it rouses, it flies, it shines, it runs,
> It burns, it lights up, it kills, it dies, it blossoms.

(AK, 13)

The harmonic effect created by the perfect vocalic symmetry of the verbs used—every single verb ends in -ad—is impossible to convey in translation. The couplet also illustrates Iqbal's ability to describe abstract ideas in concrete, tangible terms.

Adept at describing movement, Iqbal is equally adept at describing the lack of movement, his choice of appropriate words again creating the desired effect. But this 'lack of movement' does not necessarily represent in Iqbal listless inertia or bland stasis; it signifies either serene calm (in contrast to maddening and pointless hustle and bustle) or permanence and agelessness (in contrast to transientness and perishability). The 'lack of movement' in both senses is memorably depicted in the opening lines of 'Cordova Mosque', in which a predominance of multisyllabic noun-strings creates the impression of stillness on the one hand and of persistence through time on the other (the slow, measured movement of these lines invites comparison with the fast-paced movement generated by the predominance of short, mostly disyllabic, verbs in the couplet about *khudi* quoted above):

> The chain of day and night, the fashioner of events;
> The chain of day and night, the fount of life and death;
> The chain of day and night, the two-coloured yarn of silk,
> With which Being makes its coat of Attributes;
> The chain of day and night, the lament of the eternal flute,
> By means of which Being displays
> The rhythm of the Possibles—
> It puts you to the test, and it puts me to the test.
> The chain of day and night is the money-changer of the universe:
> If you come up short, or if I come up short,
> Death will be your pageant, death will be my pageant.

(BJ, 385)

Iqbal has coined many new and striking expressions. Addressing the readers of *Zarb-i Kalim* at the beginning of the book, he says that only firm resolve and determined action, and not an easy-going and comfort-loving attitude, will enable one to meet the hard challenges of life. Nature, Iqbal remarks, is *lahu-tarang*, not *jal-tarang*. *Jal-tarang* is a musical instrument that consists of a set of water-filled bowls whose edges are struck to produce notes. *Jal* means 'water', *lahu* means 'blood'. If nature is *lahu-tarang* (Iqbal's coinage) rather than *jal-tarang*, then it is a musical instrument that consists of bowls that contain blood rather than water, and it takes courage and determination to play the instrument. In another example, referring to Karl Marx's significance in the secular Western culture, Iqbal, alluding to Qur'an 7. 143—which says that God manifested Himself on Mount Sinai when Moses expressed his wish to see Him—calls the author of hallowed Communist works 'Moses without an epiphany, Jesus without a cross' (*AHu*, 650).

Iqbal frequently employs technical Islamic terms, adapting them to his poetic needs. The phrase *ummu l-kitab* literally means 'Mother of the Book'. It is used in the Qur'an in two senses: the Preserved Tablet, the repository of all knowledge, which rests with God (13. 39; 43. 4), and the foundational verses of the Islamic Scripture (3. 7). Contrasting knowledge with love (see Chapter 2) and assigning primacy to the latter, Iqbal says: 'Knowledge is the child of the Book, Love is the Mother of the Book' (*ZK*, 483). The original for 'the child of the Book' is *ibnu l-kitab* (Iqbal's coinage), which makes a nice correlative to *ummu l-kitab*. The Twelver Shi'is believe that the last of the twelve divinely designated imams is alive but in a state of occultation. Two stages of occultation are distinguished, minor and major. At first, the imam was believed to have gone into hiding (in 874) for a short period of time, at the end of which he was expected to make his appearance; this temporary disappearance is known as *ghaybat-i sughra* (minor occultation). Since the imam did not appear at the end of that period, he was believed to have gone into hiding for a longer period of time, this period, called *ghaybat-i kubra* (major occultation) still continuing. In his elegy on Sir Ross Masood, grandson of the Indian reformer Sir Sayyid Ahmad Khan, Iqbal wonders about the phenomena of life and death. Is death, he asks, *ghaybat-i sughra* (a temporary disappearance) or *fana'* (complete extinction) (*AHu*, 667)? To take another example, *khabar* and *nazar* are technical terms in certain contexts: *khabar*, literally 'report', denotes historical narration, referring especially to the body of Islamic knowledge that has been relayed from the Prophet Muhammad by a chain of transmitters through the ages. But sometimes the word acquires the somewhat pejorative connotation of derivative, intellectual knowledge or of information whose accuracy depends on the reporting of fallible individuals making up the chain of transmission. Thus, mystics contrast *khabar* with *nazar*, which literally means 'sight', but which then comes to signify direct, immediate perception or special insight and—also—the accomplished master's look that teaches a disciple more than a hundred books could. This background will explain what Iqbal means when he addresses today's Muslim in the following words:

> Intellect possesses nothing except *khabar*,
> Whereas your cure lies only in *nazar*.

(BJ, 339)

What makes Iqbal's diction quite difficult for the ordinary reader and highly challenging but most rewarding for the patient scholar is its referential and allusive character. Iqbal, as Iran's Poet Laureate Muhammad Taqi Bahar (1886–1951) remarked, is heir to a thousand years of Islamic cultural heritage. This heritage finds a powerful artistic reflection in Iqbal's poetry through the instruments of reference and allusion. Consider, for example, the following couplet:

> I lack the grace of Moses, you lack the style of Abraham—
> I have lost my life to the Samaritan's magic, you to Azar's
> blandishments.

(BD, 252)

Moses and Abraham stand for monotheism, whereas the Samaritan (according to Qur'an 25. 85–8, he made a calf for the Israelites' worship during Moses' absence) and Azar, Abraham's father (according to Qur'an 6. 74, a maker of idols), represent polytheism. Iqbal is saying that neither he nor his addressee are true monotheists (the implication is that very few Muslims are); that, despite their profession of faith in the One God, the Muslims,

as a rule, have fallen victim to the seductive charms of polytheism
and have given over their souls to idol-makers.

Or take the following couplet:

> The knowledge of things is 'He taught the names';
> It is both the staff and the shining hand.

(PM, 189)

The first hemistich quotes from Qur'an 2. 31, which says that
God 'taught Adam the names—all of them'. The verse occurs
in the context of God's installation of Adam as His deputy and
His teaching of the names of all things to Adam. According to
the commentators, to be able to name something is to have power
over it, and so God, in teaching Adam the names of all things,
gave him power over all things. In other words, knowledge is power.
The second hemistich alludes to two of the miracles of Moses
mentioned in the Qur'an: when Moses threw down his staff, it
turned into a serpent (7. 107); when he brought forth his hand
from his garment, it looked shining white (7. 108). God granted
these miracles to Moses in order to enable him to face a tough
opponent, Pharaoh. Iqbal means to say that, like Moses, knowledge
can work miracles; it has the power of Moses' staff and his shining
hand, with which it can defeat the Pharoah of ignorance.

II. IMAGERY

The sources of Iqbal's imagery are diverse. A large number of
the images are drawn from nature—the stream, the river, and
the ocean; the sky, the horizon, and the glow of sunrise or sunset;
the mountain and the valley; the field and the desert; the cloud
and the dew; the light of the sun, moon, and stars; the garden,
the nightingale, and the rose; the leopard, the eagle, and the glow-
worm; and the fire, the flame, and the spark. Iqbal also uses many
conventional images of Persian and Urdu love poetry—the female
beloved's curly tresses, the wine and the cup-bearer, and the candle
and the moth. Another category is made up of images taken from
Islamic religious and literary sources, especially the Qur'an. But

no matter what type of images he employs, Iqbal usually recasts them, giving them a new dimension of meaning.

To begin with, the sheer novelty of Iqbal's imagery is striking. Here is a stanza from 'The Himalayas':

The lightning on the mountain peaks
Has handed the clouds a whip,
With which to drive the steed of the wind.
Himalayas, are you some playground
That nature has made for the elements?
Oh, how joyous are the clouds as they reel along—
Flying away like an elephant unchained!

(BD, 22)

These lines draw three images in epic style. The first three lines (two in the original text) paint a complete picture: the wind is the swift horse, the clouds are the rider, and the lightning bolt is the whip in the rider's hand. The next two lines bring to the reader's mind the clash of the elemental forces of nature in a primal setting of vast proportions. The last two lines suggest a scene that the people of India can easily relate to—an unchained elephant stomping through the streets of a city, creating an awesome sight. In another stanza in the same poem, the Himalayas are compared to 'a book of poems with the sky as its opening couplet' and the snow on its summit is likened to 'the turban of honour, which laughs at the crown of the world-brightening sun'. These, too, are evocative images. To say that the Himalayas are like a book of poetry whose very first couplet is the sky is to say that the smallest peak of the Himalayas is as lofty as the sky and that the other peaks (the rest of the 'couplets' in the 'book of poetry') are even higher—a fine example of hyperbole. And, in several traditional Muslim societies, enturbanment of a man represents conferral of honour or recognition of merit (for example, one may receive a turban in a ritual ceremony while inheriting a spiritual authority or earning a diploma in a traditional educational institution). The Himalayas' bright white—because snowy—'turban' of honour puts to shame the glittering crown worn by the sun;

the Himalayas, in other words, proudly challenge the sovereignty of the sun.

Very often, Iqbal illustrates his thought by means of a series of diverse images used in quick succession. Of the numerous examples found in Iqbal's poetry, we will take only one. In *Asrar-i Khudi*, while explaining how *khudi*, in its search for perfection, sacrifices one level of achievement in the interest of a higher one, Iqbal mentions, among other things, the famed musk deer of the Khutan district in Turkestan, the Persian legend of Shirin's lover Farhad (who, in order to win Shirin, dug a passage through the mountains to let milk flow through it), the Pen of Destiny, and Abraham's ordeal of fire as related in the Qur'an. The pronoun 'it' in the first line refers to *khudi*:

> For the sake of a single rose, it bleeds a hundred gardens to death,
> And for the sake of a single song, it makes a hundred laments.
> It adorns the single sky with a hundred crescents,
> And creates, for the sake of a single word, a hundred discourses.
> The excuse for such extravagance—and stoneheartedness—
> Is creation and perfection of spiritual norms.
> Shirin's beauty justifies the mountain-digger's suffering,
> And a single musk justifies the death of a hundred deer of Khutan.
> Constant burning is the lot of moths—
> The candle being the justification of the moths' ordeal.
> Its pen draws a hundred todays,
> So that it may bring forth the morn of tomorrow.
> Its flames burnt up a hundred Abrahams,
> That it might light up the lamp of Muhammad.

(AK, 13)

Here, in almost every case, Iqbal makes a creative use of the image in question. For example, Qur'an 21. 68–69 relates how the king of Abraham's time had Abraham thrown into a fire, but the fire, instead of burning Abraham, became a source of comfort to him. Iqbal puts a different spin on the Qur'anic passage: the incident involving Abraham and the fire is significant in religious history, but the order of achievement represented by Abraham's fire (as

Iqbal calls it) must be transcended by another—that represented
by Muhammad's lamp—Muhammad being the final prophet and
his message being the final message from God.

An example will illustrate Iqbal's use of historical images. In
'Reply to the Complaint', Iqbal responds to the argument presented
in the earlier poem 'Complaint'—the argument, namely, that God
has not dealt too well by Muslims, who strove so hard over the
centuries to convey God's final dispensation to the entire world—
God says to Iqbal, or rather, to the Muslim of Iqbal's day:

You are a Joseph—and one, to whom every Egypt is Canaan.

By the early twentieth century, Muslims in many parts of the
world had come under colonial rule; like Joseph, who had been
taken from Canaan and sold into slavery in Egypt, Muslims were
living in a state of subjection, their native lands having become,
so to speak, foreign to them—their Canaan having become Egypt.
But Joseph's remarkable character not only won him freedom
from slavery, but also made him the master of Egypt. In the
line quoted above, Iqbal holds out the hope that, provided they
display Joseph's qualities in the difficult circumstances in which
they find themselves, the Muslims, too, can transform their situation
completely and become masters of their fate: they can not only
put an end to their servitude, they can become sovereigns of
the world, turning an 'Egypt' (where they are in a state of slavery)
into a 'Canaan' (their homeland). If we bear in mind that Iqbal
rejected the idea of territorial nationalism and envisioned the
world's Muslims as a unified community, the force of the word
'every' in the line will be brought out fully: not only a particular
country called Egypt, but 'every Egypt'—that is, every foreign
country—can become the Muslims' homeland; as Iqbal says in
a well-known line, 'We are Muslims, and the whole world is our
homeland' (BD, 159; see Chapter 5, Section II). In likening the
Muslim community to the prophet Joseph, Iqbal implies that it
is basically a good community—it is innocent and virtuous like
Joseph—and that its mission is prophetic in nature. Finally, Iqbal

is predicting a bright future for Muslims despite the heavy odds they face. We can see how a single line of poetry, drawing on sacred scriptures, makes reference to the past, present, and future of the Muslims and gives them a message of comfort and hope, at the same time charging them with the responsibility of acting, like Joseph, with wisdom and integrity.

Iqbal excels in delineation of character. Some of his finest images project the ideal human personality. Qur'an 48. 29 says that Muhammad and his followers are *ashidda'u 'ala l-kuffari ruhama'u baynahum*. The first phrase, *ashidda'u 'ala l-kuffar*, is usually translated 'hard against the unbelievers', but the underlying Arabic construction *shadidun 'ala* really means not 'one who is hard against' others, but 'one who is difficult to take advantage of'; the second phrase, *ruhama'u baynahum*, means 'kind and compassionate to one another'. This verse seems to have made a deep impact on Iqbal, for in several places, he restates its content, or rather, recasts it from his peculiar perspective. *Zarb-i Kalim* alone has three images representing the view of Muslim character stated in the Qur'anic verse. In one place, Iqbal says that the true believer can be soft and gentle in one set of circumstances but tough and rugged in another:

> In the company of friends, he is soft and gentle like silk;
> But in the clash between truth and falsehood, the believer is
>   like steel.   (ZK, 507)

Another image expresses the same idea:

> He is the dew that cools the tulip's heart;
> He is the tempest that strikes terror in the ocean's heart.
>   (ZK, 502)

Here is yet another variation:

> In war he is fiercer than the lions of the wild;
> In peace he is charming like the gazelle of Tartary.
>   (ZK, 633)

Many of Iqbal's images have symbolic import. A key symbol used by him is that of the tulip, a flower that has such a strong personality that it would grow even in the inhospitable environment of a desert. The flower thus becomes an attractive model—even a role model—to Iqbal, who wants Muslims to cultivate their *khudi*, to rely on themselves to solve their problems, and to carve out their own destiny in the face of odds and difficulties. The falcon or eagle in Iqbal's poetry possesses the qualities that are necessary for success in life: it has a sharp vision; it takes delight in action; it relies on its own ability to catch its prey, which it pursues with total concentration; and it likes to live in a free environment. The bird, thus, comes to symbolize freedom, self-reliance, action, and contentment—and, as such, deserves to be emulated. Several of Iqbal's poems deal exclusively with the falcon. In one of them, an old falcon gives the following advice to its young one:

> You know that, in essence, all falcons are one—
> A mere handful of feathers, but with the heart of a lion.
> Conduct yourself well, and let your strategy be well considered;
> Be daring, maintain your dignity, and hunt big game.
> Do not mix with partridge, pheasant, and starling—
> Unless you want them as prey.
> What a lowly, fearful lot they are—
> They wipe their beaks clean with dust!
> A falcon that copies the ways of its prey
> Becomes a prey itself.
> Many a predator, descending to earth,
> Has perished on associating with grain-eaters.
> Guard yourself, and live the life
> Of one of good cheer, brave, robust, and rugged.
> Let the quail have its soft and delicate body;
> Grow a vein hard as a deer's horn.
> All the joy in the world
> Comes from hardship, toil, and fullness of breath.
>
> (PM, 272)

Iqbal's images bear an integral relation to his thought. Even when he uses conventional images, Iqbal gives them a different slant, extending their application or reinterpreting them, thus adapting them to his purposes. Take, for example, the image of the bubble, which in Persian and Urdu poetry represents ephemeral existence: poets frequently liken the transience of life or the pleasures of life to a bubble. Iqbal, who teaches that human beings must preserve their *khudi* under all circumstances, uses the image of the bubble to a completely different end. In *Asrar-i Khudi*, in the concluding couplet of the section entitled 'Petitioning Weakens Khudi', the bubble comes to symbolize independence:

> Let your manly dignity turn you into a bubble:
> Even in an ocean, let your cup be overturned.

> (AK, 24)

That is, even in a situation of abundant resources (as in a sea), where petitioning for something can get you more than what you need, turn over your cup, signifying refusal to accept handouts, asserting your independence from the environment, and declaring your intention to survive on your own and make your own destiny. In a similar vein, Iqbal says in the Introduction to *Rumuz-i Bikhudi*:

> My neck would not come under the yoke of a favour—
> In a garden my hem becomes a bud.

> (AK, 24)

Here, too, the stock image of picking flowers from a garden and collecting them in one's hem is put to a new use: the poet has such self-respect that, even in a garden, he would not fill up his hem with flowers that have been grown by others; like a bud, his hem will close up, opening up only to gather flowers that he himself has grown.

III. NARRATIVE AND DRAMATIC ELEMENTS

Scattered throughout Iqbal's Persian and Urdu poetical works are anecdotes and stories of various kinds. Several of the poems that he adapted from other writers, such as 'A Spider and A Fly'

(*BD*, 29–30) and 'A Cow and a Goat' (*BD*, 32–4), retell children's tales. A number of poems are about actual events in Islamic history. For example, 'The Truthful One' (*BD*, 224–5) shows that Muhammad's trusted Companion, Abu Bakr, known as 'the Truthful One', was not to be outdone by anyone when it came to making sacrifices in the cause of Islam. 'The Siege of Adrianople' (*BD*, 216) narrates how, during the Second Balkan War (1913), the besieged Turkish general Shukri Pasha was forced by the verdict of the city's Muslim religious scholars to retract, even in a state of emergency, his orders to confiscate food supplies belonging to non-Muslims. In some cases, Iqbal chooses the medium of story to present his ideas. For example, 'The Story of Adam' (*BD*, 81–2), which sums up major achievements made by human beings in history, expresses Iqbal's faith in the enterprising and irrepressible human spirit, whereas 'Love' (*BD*, 111–2) suggests that love is the glue that holds the universe together.

But the most sustained use of narrative in Iqbal occurs in those long Persian poems in which he relates stories to illustrate key points of his philosophic thought. Take, for example, his concept of *khudi* as stated in *Asrar-i Khudi*. To illustrate his view that the doctrine of negation of *khudi* is a ploy used by the dominant nations to keep the weaker nations in subjection, Iqbal relates a fable: a herd of sheep, constantly under attack by a pride of lions, convinced the latter that true merit lay in cultivating spiritual rather than physical power, with the result that the lions, having lost their ability to hunt, were reduced to pitiable weaklings (*AK*, 28–31). To show that challenge strengthens *khudi*, Iqbal tells the story of a young man who visited the great saint 'Ali Hujwiri (d. 1072) and complained to him that he was unable to fend off the many enemies that surrounded him. The saint, instead of commiserating with the young man, remarked that a powerful enemy is a blessing from God since such an enemy presents a man with challenges that push him to the limit, thereby bringing out the best in him (*AK*, 52–3). *Rumuz-i Bikhudi*, the companion volume to *Asrar-i Khudi*, also relates a number of stories. But it is *Jawid-Namah* that contains the most impressive display of Iqbal's narrative skills. The long poem narrates the poet's travels, under Rumi's guidance, through heavenly spheres. History, myth, allegory, personification, and imaginative reconstruction combine to make *Jawid-Namah* a masterpiece of world literature.

Iqbal's poetry has a strong dramatic element. To begin with, Iqbal frequently uses the device of dialogue. Many of his poems have the structure of a dialogue—for example, 'Reason and Heart' (*BD*, 41–2), which compares the merits of reason and intuition, according preference to the latter. 'The Moth and the Glow-Worm' (*BJ*, 407) presents the glow-worm favourably, since, unlike the moth, which circles an alien light, it has a light it can call its own. 'The Ant and the Eagle' (*BJ*, 461) says that the ant is wretched because it searches for food in the earth's dusty paths, whereas the eagle enjoys a lofty status because it soars higher than the heavens—making the point that one creates one's own destiny.

Several of Iqbal's poems are conceived roughly like plays. 'Conquest of Nature' (*PM*, 255–8) depicts, in broad outline, the drama of Adam's creation, his deception by Iblis, and his reconciliation with God (for a detailed discussion, see Mir, *Tulip in the Desert*, pp. 21–34). Another poem in this category is 'Iblis's Advisory Council' (*AHu*, 647–53). In his opening speech, Iblis (Satan), claims to be the unchallenged sovereign of the world. His advisors voice concerns that the Iblisic system, which has divided humankind into masters and slaves, may be threatened by such philosophies and systems as democracy, fascism, and communism. After some discussion has taken place among the advisors, Satan delivers his concluding address, in which he discounts all the aforementioned dangers, saying that the only worrisome prospect is the resurgence of Islam, a religion that, according to him, furnishes human beings with a moral basis of unity, creating a just and egalitarian system that would put an end to the political oppression, social inequality, and economic disparity generated by the Iblisic system. The poem is dramatic not only in respect of its form, but also in respect of the psychological study it provides of Iblis. Iblis's inaugural speech is meant to assure his advisors that he is firmly in control of the world situation. By the end of the proceedings, however, Iblis has shown himself to be vulnerable, and the reassurance he held out to his advisors is seen to hide a deep insecurity: not only does the plot thicken as the poem progresses, but dramatic revelation of character also takes place.

'Gabriel and Iblis' (BJ, 435–6), too, is also interesting as a study in character. Gabriel and Iblis happen to meet a long time after Iblis's expulsion from the heavens on account of his refusal to obey the Divine command to bow before Adam. Gabriel asks how the terrestrial world, to which Iblis has been banished, is, and Iblis responds in words that indicate both regret and pain: 'Burning and suffering, scars and pain, seeking and longing!' But when Gabriel asks him if there is any chance of his making restitution and regaining his lost status in the eyes of God, Iblis begins to puff with pride, for he now recalls the consequential—and fateful—role he played in the drama of creation and, subsequently, in the life of human beings on earth. His mood visibly changed, Iblis rejects the idea of trying to make amends for his sin. (For more details, see Mir, *Tulip in the Desert*, pp. 35–9.)

IV. FOLDS OF MEANING

Rumi's *Mathnawi* has been called the Qur'an in Persian. It is often said that, if the Qur'an had to be revealed in Urdu, it would have been revealed in Iqbal's Urdu. To say that Iqbal's language is fit to be the language of scripture is to say, in part, that his language, like scripture's language, is a deep quarry of meaning. To those who look for a 'combination of strength and elegance, of deep content and attractive form' (Schimmel, 'Iqbal's Persian Poetry', in Yarshater, *Persian Literature*, p. 427), Iqbal's poetry gives, to borrow a New Testament image, 'a good measure, pressed down, shaken together, and running over' (Luke 6:38). The analogy between scripture and Iqbal's poetry cannot, of course, be pushed too far. It is nevertheless true that many dimensions of Iqbal's poetry remain unexplored. Here, I would like to draw attention to a certain literary feature of that poetry.

Iqbal's poetry has what may be called folds of meaning. His verses, that is to say, yield their full meaning only upon close, patient study that takes into account both what they say and what they leave unsaid. Iqbal has a flair for embedding a range of meanings in a few words. The embedment consists not only in the use of allusion—of which we have already seen several examples—but also in the construction of a charged context. We will illustrate this by presenting and analysing an example in some detail.

One of the best-known of Iqbal's Urdu poems is the long 'Complaint' (BD 163–70). Iqbal has a complaint against God—to whom, also, the complaint is addressed. The poem opens with these words:

> Why must I be a loser, and be heedless of gain;
> Take no thought of tomorrow, ever grieving over yesterday;
> Listen to the nightingale's cries—and be all ears?
> Am I, fellow-singer, some rose that must keep quiet?
> My power of speech makes me audacious:
> I have—dust in my mouth!—a complaint against God!

(BD, 163)

To those familiar with the conventions of Persian and Urdu poetry, the stanza's basic meaning will be quite clear. The speaker is a poet—as can be inferred from the word 'fellow-singer'—and he wishes to make a complaint against God. Since his complaint is against God, the speaker must somehow think that God is responsible for the state of affairs that generates the complaint. The poet is reluctant to grieve over the past—which, in order for the grieving to make sense, must have been remarkable. Since the poet contrasts his glorious 'yesterday' with his uncertain 'tomorrow', his 'today', we can safely infer, is not enviable either. In brief, he is nostalgic about his past, dissatisfied with his present, and apprehensive about his future. He is, however, unwilling to accept the situation in which he finds himself. Likening himself to a songbird in a garden, the poet says that he finds it hard to contain himself when he hears the nightingale's lament. Had he been a rose, he might have kept quiet, but he is aware of his ability to sing—to express himself effectively, that is—and so he will use his elocutionary skills to represent those who are suffering but have no one to speak for them. By now, it should be clear that the garden represents the Muslim community, and that the poet has decided to serve as its spokesperson.

A closer study of the stanza will show it to have several 'folds of meaning', and the language of the stanza, which appears to have the quality of extemporaneity, will be seen to be nuanced and imbued with deep meaning—and, thus, to have been crafted with great artistic skill. Consider the following points:

1. The stanza begins with three questions, taking up the first three lines. It is not until we reach line 4 that we learn that there is a fellow-singer (that is, a fellow-poet) to whom the speaker's questions are addressed. The abrupt and pointed nature of the questions in lines 1–3 suggests that the questions are in response to something that the fellow-poet has said, and that a conversation between the two has already been going on for some time. Presumably, the poet has expressed to his fellow-poet his intention of complaining against the wretched condition of his community, and the fellow-poet, considering this a bad idea or an impolitic step, makes an unsuccessful attempt to dissuade the poet from doing so. The poet's ambivalent attitude towards his fellow-poet is worth noting. He feels the need to justify to the latter his decision to speak up, even though the fellow-poet cannot stop him from venting his grievance. At the same time, he carefully distinguishes himself from his fellow-poet, who, in his view, belongs to the group of people who have resigned themselves to the existing situation and would do nothing to alter it for reasons of expediency, from a lack of hope or sense of responsibility, or simply owing to indifference. Both the speaker (Iqbal) and his fellow-poet have the ability to raise the consciousness of their community, but only Iqbal has chosen to use his ability to that end. Iqbal, in other words, criticizes his fellow-poets—or the generality of Muslim

intellectuals—for their apathetic attitude towards the Muslim community's affairs and for their failure to discharge their proper role in society.

The reference to the fellow-poet in line 4 imparts a dramatic quality to the opening of 'Complaint'. For, not only this line, but the entire stanza is now read as an address to the fellow-poet. The series of questions beginning in line 1 acquires cumulative force, becoming a powerful rejoinder to the fellow-poet's implied counsel to Iqbal to keep silent.

2. We have already noted that, since the poet's complaint is against God, he must believe that God is, in some sense, responsible for the Muslim community's sad state. If we bear in mind that the essence of the complaint is the contrast of 'yesterday' with 'tomorrow'—and also with 'today'—we should be able to figure out that the Muslim community has, in the poet's estimation, fallen from grace: God is no longer as favourably disposed to the community as He was in previous ages. The poet does realize the gravity of the idea of making a complaint against God, and so he utters an appropriate 'Dust in my mouth!', an idiomatic expression intended as an apology for making a possibly blasphemous remark. Even though it is uttered politely and circumspectly, the phrase here serves as a theological postscript: the reader cannot but conclude that, according to the poet, while Muslims have served God faithfully, God has allowed them to suffer in several ways, instead of rewarding them for their devoted and selfless service. The Muslims have a feeling that God has let them down, and Iqbal wishes to voice that feeling.

3. The stanza gives three reasons why Iqbal feels compelled to express himself.

First, there is the pragmatic reason: to remain silent in the face of suffering will perpetuate the suffering; the only hope for amelioration lies in making a protest. To remain silent is to incur a loss, whereas to speak up is to make a legitimate effort to improve one's lot (line 1). A word may be said about the two main phrases in line 1 of the original—*ziyan-kar* (literally, one whose actions produce a loss—hence, one who makes a losing deal) and *sud-faramosh* (one who is heedless of, or indifferent to, one's gain). *Sud* (profit, gain) and *ziyan* (loss) have special connotations in Iqbal's vocabulary: as a rule, they stand, respectively, for worldly gain and worldly loss as determined by calculating reason. The use of the two phrases in line 1, thus, has an ironic potential: by expressing his resolve not to become *ziyan-kar* or *sud-faramosh*, the speaker unwittingly provides an argument against himself. He says, in effect, that he views mundane success and failure as decisive— an admission that will be used by God in 'Reply to the Complaint' as a basis for His counter-argument against the poet—and, through him, against the Muslims (*BD*, 199–208).

Second, it is part of being human to react to suffering and attempt to overcome it. Humans, after all, are not passive beings that are, like a tongue-tied plant, resigned to determination of their lot by outside forces (line 4). By nature, they wish to change their condition for the better. The intelligent ones among them do not dwell on the past, grieving over their past losses, but seek to build a bright future for themselves (line 2). In other words, consciousness—the distinctive human possession—imposes on human beings the responsibility to take stock of their situation and make every effort to improve it.

Third, Iqbal feels that he bears a special responsibility to articulate himself: he has been blessed with the gift of speech (in line 5 of the original, the phrase *tab-i sukhan*, which in other contexts may mean 'courage to speak', means 'ability to speak'. Aware that he can compose eloquent poetry (the word *sukhan*, literally 'speech, discourse', here also has the specific connotation of 'poetry', *tab-i sukhan* thus signifying 'poetic skill'), Iqbal feels an even keener sense of responsibility to represent his community, and so he makes bold to speak. He realizes that his boldness verges on insolence, but express himself he must. And so, with a proper apology (line 6), he states the thesis of his poem: he has a complaint against God.

We can now summarize the meaning of the stanza: As a singer in the garden (that is, as a poet of the Muslim community), Iqbal hears the nightingale pining for the rose (that is, he learns of the suffering of his people), and he finds it hard to remain silent. For he not only thinks of the community's past—a glorious past, the loss of which alone is sufficient to keep him grieving over it—but also has an eye to the future—he hopes and wishes to improve their lot. He is conscious, furthermore, that he has been given the power of speech, that he can express himself rather eloquently, and this awareness imposes a special obligation on him: he must represent his community and help it voice its concern— before none other than God Himself!

In this section, we have looked at only one example—and that from Iqbal's Urdu poetry. A study of Iqbal's Persian poetry (and Iqbal's Urdu poetry itself is highly Persianized) will show that it, too, has rich—perhaps richer—folds of meaning. Ehsan Yarshater's evaluation will come as no surprise to students of Persian literature: 'Iqbal may well be considered the most significant poet in the classical Persian tradition since Hafez [d. 1390]' (Yarshater, in Yarshater, p. 31).

4

Philosophical Thought

We will discuss two works of Iqbal: *The Development of Metaphysics in Persia: A Contribution to the History of Muslim Philosophy* and *The Reconstruction of Religious Thought in Islam*. The first is Iqbal's doctoral thesis, presented to Munich University in 1907. The second consists of seven lectures. After reviewing the *Metaphysics* briefly, we will focus our attention on the *Reconstruction*, which represents Iqbal's mature philosophical thought.

I. THE DEVELOPMENT OF METAPHYSICS IN PERSIA

The view that the *Metaphysics*, once a significant piece of scholarship, is now mostly of academic interest, is only partly correct. Some of the statements in the book lack historical accuracy, and some of the views presented in it are not original and reflect European treatments of the book's subject-matter. But scholarship can still benefit from Iqbal's account of the thought of several thinkers and writers. Iqbal's comparative notes about Muslim and Western thinkers still provide useful leads for future scholarship. And, of course, the book still needs to be studied in more detail— and from more than one angle—in the larger context of the development of Iqbal's own thought. (The *Metaphysics* documents, for example, Iqbal's preoccupation with, or preference for, the Sufi doctrine of *wahdat al-wujud*, or existential monism.)

Iqbal dedicates the work to Thomas Arnold, his mentor in India and in England: 'This little book is the first fruit of that literary and philosophical training which I have been receiving from you for the last ten years.' In the Introduction, Iqbal states the scope of the work: he will attempt, first, 'to trace the logical continuity of Persian thought . . . in the language of modern Philosophy', and, second, to show that 'Sufiism is a necessary product of the play of various intellectual and moral forces which would necessarily awaken the slumbering soul to a higher ideal of life' (xi).

The Metaphysics deals with a historical subject, divided into two parts. Part I, 'Pre-Islamic Persian Philosophy', presents the teachings of Zoroaster, Mani, and Mazdak. Part II, 'Greek Dualism', has five chapters: 'Neo-Platonic Aristotelians of Persia', 'Islamic Rationalism', 'Controversy between Realism and Idealism', 'Sufiism', and 'Later Persian Thought'. There is a brief concluding chapter. Iqbal envisaged the Metaphysics as 'a ground-work for a future history of Persian Metaphysics' (p. xi). Considering the state of scholarship at the time at which it was written, the Metaphysics is a highly informative and illuminating work. Iqbal offers summaries—often detailed and always succinct—of the views and doctrines of a number of important religious, theological, philosophical, and mystic figures, including Zoroaster (pp. 3–11), Ibn Miskawayh (pp. 23–37), the Ash'arite school of theologians (pp. 52–64), Shihab al-Din al-Suhrawardi (pp. 96–116), 'Abd al-Karim al-Jili (pp. 116–33), Mulla Hadi of Sabzwar (p. 135), and 'Ali Muhammad Bab of Shiraz (pp. 143–6).

Iqbal competently deals with the available research resources in English and German as well as in Arabic and Persian. For his account of pre-Islamic Iranian thought, he relies heavily on Western resources (he acknowledges the debt in the Introduction), but he makes a direct study of a fairly large number of primary resources, including some manuscripts he was able to find in British and German libraries. Iqbal is probably the first writer to have drawn attention to the significance of Mulla Sadra and Mulla Hadi of Sabzwar in the post-classical period of Muslim philosophy.

Although mainly a historical account, the *Metaphysics* furnishes evidence not only of Iqbal's wide-ranging scholarship, but also of his originality of thought. In analysing the rise and growth of Sufism, for example, Iqbal rejects the prevalent view, namely, that Muslim mysticism owes its origin to non-Islamic influences (pp. 76–7). Given the pervasiveness and deep roots of Sufism in Islam, such views are mistaken, for

No idea can seize a people's soul unless, in some sense, it is the people's own. External influences may wake it up from its deep unconscious slumber; but they cannot, so to speak, create it out of nothing. . . . The full significance of a phenomenon in the intellectual evolution of a people can only be comprehended in the light of those pre-existing intellectual, political, and social conditions which alone make its existence inevitable. (pp. 76–7)

Iqbal then proceeds to give details of the background of Sufism, enumerating a set of six conditions that led to the rise of mystical tendencies in early Islam: political unrest, the sceptical outlook of the Muslim Rationalists, the unemotional piety of the Islamic legal schools, theological controversies, the softening of religious fervour due to intellectualism and the moral laxity due to economic affluence, and the influence of the Christian ideal of life (pp. 77–80). Iqbal's view remains largely valid today, as is his explanation of the 'extraordinary vitality of the Sufi restatement of Islam' (p. 82):

It would, therefore, be evident that the secret of the vitality of Sufism is the complete view of human nature upon which it is based. It has survived orthodox persecutions and political revolutions, because it appeals to human nature in its entirety; and, while it concentrates its interest chiefly on a *life* of self-denial, it allows free play to the speculative tendency as well. (p. 83)

The *Metaphysics* demonstrates Iqbal's ability to compare Eastern and Western thinkers and to note similarities in their thought. Thus, he compares Zoroaster with Plato and Schopenhauer (p. 7), Mani with the Indian thinker Kapila and with the German philosophers Leibniz and Schopenhauer (p. 14–5), and 'Abd al-Karim al-Jili with Schleiermacher (p. 123). At times, he sums up, with almost epigrammatic force, similar currents of thought in different cultures, for example: 'The outcome of all Idealistic speculation in India is Buddha, in Persia Bahaullah, and in the West Schopenhauer, whose system, in Hegelian language, is the marriage of free oriental universality with occidental determinateness' (p. x). Although a short treatise, the *Metaphysics* elicited praise from several experts in the field of Islamic studies, including Edward G. Browne and Reynold Nicholson.

II. THE RECONSTRUCTION OF RELIGIOUS THOUGHT IN ISLAM

The Reconstruction of Religious Thought in Islam, Iqbal's philosophical *magnum opus*, still awaits a detailed study. The seven lectures of the book bear the mark of a brilliant intellect that is seriously engaged with the vast and diverse Western and Islamic philosophical and literary traditions, offering a keen analysis of issues and often presenting an original synthesis of ideas.

Iqbal's aim in the book is to meet 'the demand for a scientific form of religious knowledge . . . by attempting to reconstruct Muslim religious philosophy with due regard to the philosophical tradition of Islam and the more recent developments in the various domains of human knowledge' (pp. xxi-ii). In his view, the modern mind, with its 'habits of concrete thought', is unable to re-live 'that special type of inner experience on which religious faith ultimately rests' (p. xxi), and so it needs to be approached on terms that are familiar to it. Furthermore, Muslims ought to take a positive, if critical, attitude towards modern developments in the field of knowledge (p. xxii). Sufism once did 'good work in shaping and directing the evolution of religious experience in Islam', but its 'latter-day representatives, owing to their ignorance of the modern mind, have become absolutely incapable of receiving any fresh inspiration from modern thought and experience', and are consequently unable to offer a method suited to the modern mind (p. xxi). It is this deficiency that Iqbal hopes to supply to some extent. He is hopeful that, with a self-critical physics calling the early form of materialism in question, 'the day is not far off when Religion and Science may discover hitherto unsuspected mutual harmonies' (pp. xxi-ii).

In accepting as legitimate 'the demand for a scientific form of religious knowledge' and the challenge to make Islam accessible to the modern, scientific mind, Iqbal parts company with two Muslim groups of colonial India. The first consists of those traditionally minded Muslim scholars who, being unwilling or unable to engage with modernity, were content with a world-view of Islam that had changed little since medieval times. The second consists of those secularly minded Muslim intellectuals who, being unable or unwilling to draw strength and inspiration from their own long-standing religious tradition, were only too ready to receive the baptism of Western modernity. Bearing in mind the attitudes of these two groups will help us to appreciate the importance of Iqbal's project and to understand accurately his fundamental philosophical stance.

Iqbal distinguishes between religious faith and theological method. Religious faith, which depends on a 'special type of inner experience', may be likened to spirit, whereas theological method, which explains and rationalizes that faith, may be called the form assumed by that spirit. While religious faith is a constant, theological method has a certain contingency about it: it develops in response to issues raised by the peculiar habits of thought in a given age, and it requires revision or replacement if those habits change in a later era. In Iqbal's view, the classical structures of Muslim thought and spirituality are incapable of making an effective response to the issues raised by the modern mind's penchant for concrete thought, and this fact underscores the need for a reconstruction of Muslim religious philosophy. Such reconstruction comes under the general heading of *tajdid*, the Islamic technical term for a significant 'renewal' or 'rejuvenation' of Islamic religion. Iqbal's *Reconstruction* itself may be viewed as a contribution to the cause of Islamic *tajdid*.

Although Iqbal hopes that religion and science, now estranged from each other, will one day find common ground, one cannot help feeling that Iqbal regards the modern mind's incapability of reliving religious experience as an impoverishment, or even as a disability. One of Iqbal's Indian Muslim predecessors, Sayyid Ahmad Khan, sought to bridge the gap between religion and science by putting science on a high pedestal and requiring religion to adjust to scientific desiderata. Iqbal has been called a continuator of Sayyid Ahmad Khan's intellectual legacy in this respect. But, considering Iqbal's view that the scientific mind would do well to relive religious experience, he can hardly be described in these terms. The brilliance of Iqbal's intellectual argument in the *Reconstruction* can blind the reader to the fact that a singeing passion, born of a profound vision of Islam as a system of thought and practice, informs that argument.

In attempting a reconstruction of Muslim religious thought, Iqbal would pay 'due regard' both to the Islamic philosophical tradition and to the modern developments in knowledge. This promise is carried out by Iqbal quite faithfully, as our review of the *Reconstruction* will show. We will divide our review into two parts. The first part will, by summarising the individual lectures, try to provide a much-needed overview of this admittedly difficult work; the original lecture titles will be used as subheadings in this part. The second part will offer an exposition, with comments, of some of the principal motifs and themes of the book.

A. *Lectures: Summaries*

1. 'Knowledge and Religious Experience'

Religion claims to furnish a direct vision of Reality. Religion is essentially faith, but faith has, besides feeling, a cognitive element. This is indicated by the importance of ideas in both scholastic and mystical thought and by the fact that religion, which aims to transform human life and character, anticipated science in realizing the need to base itself on a rational foundation. Religion may, therefore, be subjected to philosophical scrutiny. However, since it is not merely idea, feeling, or action, but an expression of the whole man, religion will submit to such scrutiny only on its own terms, and philosophy may not assign it an inferior position among its data. Furthermore, there is no essential difference between thought and intuition. Intuition, which approaches Reality as a whole, is only a higher form of thought, which approaches Reality piecemeal.

The Muslims' quest for a rational understanding of their religion began quite early, with both scholastics and mystics trying to build a coherent system of ideas. Under the strong influence of Greek philosophy, Muslim thinkers failed to see that, while the speculative Greek thought was distrustful of sense-perception, the Qur'an views the world as real, taking an empirical approach to its phenomena. Al-Ghazali's subsequent revolt against Greek philosophy was born of his rejection of analytic reason as a viable basis for religion, which then led him to found religion exclusively on mystic experience. But al-Ghazali's approach lacked Qur'anic sanction. Later thinkers, too, failed to see that thought and intuition, which are characterized by finitude and infinitude, respectively, are organically related—thought in its deeper movement becoming intuition. In other words, thought, which possesses internal infinitude, only simulates finitude because of its self-unfolding movement in serial time.

Muslim religious thought has been stagnant for the last five hundred years. Meanwhile, Europe, inspired by the world of Islam, has been constantly progressing in various fields, generating new ideas and viewpoints. It is time for Muslims to look to the essentials of their religion.

The Qur'an's principal aim is to deepen man's consciousness of his relations with God and the universe. Islam agrees with Christianity that elevation of human spiritual life is possible only through the revelation of a new world within man; unlike Christianity, it asserts that such revelation is not antithetical to the material world but permeates it. According to the Qur'an, the universe has a serious purpose, is capable of extension and change, contains signs of God, and holds the promise of its conquest by man. Man is superior to nature; he is meant to shape both his own destiny and nature's, rising continuously from one level to another until he becomes God's co-worker. But his life and his growth depend on his ability to establish the right relationship with the reality that confronts him, and it is knowledge—sense-perception amplified by understanding—that will enable him to establish that relationship. The Ultimate Reality reveals its symbols both in the external world and in man's inner self and may, therefore, be called the immanent Infinite. Reflective observation of nature is an indirect, rational mode of reaching that Reality; intuition is a direct, non-rational mode of reaching it. The latter mode, whose validity is attested by the world's revealed and mystic literature, is no less natural and genuine and no less effective in yielding objective, concrete, and real knowledge. The two types of knowledge must, however, supplement each other to make a complete vision of Reality possible.

Mystic knowledge is characterized by immediacy, wholeness, objectivity, and incommunicability. Though unique, it is never completely disconnected from common experience. That mystic experience occurs under certain organic conditions, or that it may be the result of the working of the sex impulse, does not diminish its value. All knowledge occurs under certain organic conditions, and religious consciousness is, in respect of its character and its objective, often significantly at variance with sexual. But mystic knowledge, like any other, needs to be clarified. Freudian psychology, though its main theory is questionable, has greatly helped in purging religious experience of subjective elements.

Two tests, one intellectual and one pragmatic, can be applied to assess the validity of religious experience. The intellectual test, applied in the next lecture, critiques human experience with a view to determining whether it will yield the same reality that religious experience yields. The pragmatic test evaluates religious experience in terms of its effects in real life.

2. 'The Philosophical Test of the Revelations of Religious Experience'

Scholastic philosophy's cosmological, teleological, and ontological arguments to prove the existence of God, the Absolute Being, are inadequate. The first argument affirms the existence of the infinite by negating the finite; the second proves the existence of an artificer, not that of a creator; and the third fails to explain how the idea of a perfect being necessarily implies the objective existence of such a being. The arguments, moreover, give a superficial account of human experience.

The ontological and theological arguments fail because they view thought as an organizing principle that works on things from without, whereas it ought to be viewed as a potency that forms the very being of its material. The dualism of thought and being, necessitated by our human situation, can be resolved into a unity through a critical interpretation of experience, following the Qur'anic lead that man's experience, both within and without, is symbolic of an Ultimate Reality.

Experience unfolds itself in time at three levels—those of matter, life, and consciousness, which are studied, respectively, by physics, biology, and psychology. The traditional theory of matter is no longer tenable. Modern physics, having reduced sensory evidence to mental impressions and 'things' to 'events', has shown all things to be essentially movement, suggesting that 'thing' is only a derivative notion. Nor is life—or consciousness, a variety of life— explicable in terms of a mechanistic physics. Thus, matter, life, and consciousness, when analysed, point to a reality that is spiritual in character, is continuously creative, and is rationally directed. In our immediate experience, too, nature appears as an unbroken continuity, which thought, for practical exigencies, breaks up into spatially isolated entities, thus turning what is a dynamic unity into mutually isolated immobile things. These immobilities, through their coexistence and succession, give rise to our space and time. In its efficient capacity, the self deals with the multiplicity of spatialized 'heres' and serial 'nows'; in its appreciative capacity, however, it synthesizes all these 'heres' and 'nows' into a single 'now' unadulterated by space. This pure time is an organic whole that includes the past, the present, and—as an open possibility rather than as an unalterable fate—the future. To exist in pure time is to be a self, an ego. The human ego arises out of the self's distinction from a confronting not-self in space—that is, from nature. The Divine or Ultimate Ego is not so confronted, as the not-self or nature is organic to it—being what the Qur'an calls God's habit, which we may interpret as the Absolute Ego's creative activity. The Absolute Ego is active and changes, but the change that may be predicated of it is intensive or qualitative, not extensive or quantitative. In other words, it is change without duration or change in real, non-serial, time.

Thus, a philosophical criticism of experience reveals, on an intellectual level, that Reality is spiritual in character, and that it must be thought of as an ego. Religion, going a step further, gives us the promise of experience of that Reality.

3. 'The Conception of God and the Meaning of Prayer'

The important elements in the Qur'anic conception of God—the Ultimate Ego—are His individuality, creativeness, knowledge, omnipotence, and eternity. The individuality of the infinite God does not imply finitude; the Divine infinity is intensive, not extensive. God's creation of nature is not to be conceived as a specific past event; matter is not an independent reality confronting God, but an interpretation that thought places on His free creative energy. Unlike the knowledge of the finite ego, which presupposes a known independent object, the knowledge of God does not have a confronting object of knowledge, but creates that object itself. Creation possesses egohood in varying degrees; only man, who possesses it in the highest degree, is capable of participating in God's creative life.

The notion of omniscience suggests a predetermined future, negating God's freedom to act and eliminating novelty from the scheme of things. Properly understood, Divine knowledge includes the future as an open possibility.

Divine omnipotence, which is closely connected in the Qur'an with Divine wisdom and goodness, seems problematic in view of the world's pervasive physical and moral evil. Qur'anic meliorism holds out the hope of man's final triumph over evil. And the Qur'anic interpretation of the Fall of Man presents man not as a depraved being, but as a being free to choose between good and evil. The freedom of the human ego implies, equally, the ego's ability to choose good or evil, and so neither good nor evil can be seen in isolation from each other, both being necessary parts of the same whole. Man's finite ego grows only by way of trial and error. Pain, therefore, may be regarded as part of the discipline man is supposed to undergo in life. The full implications of this discipline are, however, not known to man at this stage of the evolution of his ego.

The eternity of God is to be understood in terms of His existence in pure—that is, non-successional—time. Pure time appears as serial time by virtue of God's creative movement in the world of change. Permanence and change, thus, are not irreconcilable categories of time as far as God is concerned.

The foregoing shows that it is possible to justify philosophically the Islamic conception of God. But religion, not content with a philosophical understanding of God, aims at the higher goal of establishing an intimate relation with Him. Worship or prayer, which affords spiritual illumination, is the means religion employs to reach that goal. Prayer is like reflection in that both are assimilative processes. In philosophical reflection, however, the mind observes Reality, whereas in religious prayer the mind seeks to participate in the life of Reality. There is nothing mysterious about prayer: all search for knowledge is a kind of prayer. Prayer is, in fact, a necessary complement to the scientific observation of nature. A scientist observing nature is like a mystic in an act of prayer. Congregational prayer, which Islam enjoins, serves to socialize spiritual illumination. It also promotes social equality, indicating that the unity of human beings must follow from the unity of their maker and sustainer, God.

4. 'The Human Ego—His Freedom and Immortality'

The Qur'an emphasizes man's individuality and uniqueness. It calls man the one chosen by God, the would-be deputy of God on earth, and the possessor of a free personality. Surprisingly, however, consciousness, which is central to human personality, never became a serious subject with Muslim scholastics. Devotional

Sufism alone approached the unity of inner experience, recognized by the Qur'an as one of the three sources of knowledge—history and nature being the other two. The mystic Hallaj's statement 'I am the creative truth', when properly interpreted, signifies not the drop's merging into the ocean, but the subsistence of the finite human ego in a profounder being. This type of experience, in its mature form, is not yet accessible to modern psychology, but theological systems, using the language of a dead metaphysics, do not provide a clue to it either. The modern Muslim, therefore, needs to re-evaluate the legacy and teachings of Islam in the light of modern knowledge, which he must approach with a respectful but independent attitude—and without severing his connection with his own past.

The reality of the ego is undeniable, as even Bradley, who could not prove the ego's existence on logical grounds, conceded. The ego is characterized by a unity of mental states that is not bound by space (the ego's unity thus differing from a material thing's unity) or by time (the ego's time span thus differing from a physical event's time span). The ego is also characterized by privacy—which raises, for psychology, the question of the nature of the unique 'I'.

Al-Ghazali, and the theological school he represented, viewed the ego as a simple, indivisible, and immutable soul-substance and thought of man's inner experience as a unity because of the relation of his mental states to the changeless ego. That school was, however, chiefly interested in metaphysics rather than in psychology, though its theory serves neither a metaphysical purpose (since that which is indivisible is not necessarily indestructible) nor a psychological end (since our conscious experience tells us nothing about the ego viewed as a soul-substance). And yet the only access to the ego is through interpretation of our conscious experience. William James's description of consciousness as 'a stream of consciousness' is not true to our experience of consciousness as something single, permanent, and continuous.

The ego is an act, not a thing. One's personality can be

perceived only through interpretation of one's acts rather than through observation of one as if one were a thing. What is the relationship between the ego or soul and matter or body? Matter has no independent existence. A physical organism is a colony of low-order egos through which the Ultimate Ego—which is immanent in nature—operates on one's self, enabling one to collect, systematize, and unify one's experience and permitting the emergence of a higher-order ego. Life's evolution consists in the reversal of the initial domination of the physical by the mental, the latter possibly reaching a point of complete independence of the physical.

Having proceeded from a directive Ultimate or Divine Ego, the human ego, too, is directive. By the same token, the human ego is a free personal causality. *Taqdir* (destiny), an important Qur'anic concept, does not signify crass fatalism; it represents a unitive experience in which the finite ego is aligned with the Infinite Ego, the latter embracing the former without obliterating it.

Furthermore, the human ego is potentially immortal—its immortality being personal rather than collective or civilizational. The human ego is, according to the Qur'an, supposed to grow in self-possession and uniqueness, ultimately reaching the presence of the Infinite without losing its individuality. Thus, it is distinct from the Infinite without being isolated from it. The ego's growth in self-possession is made possible through action. Life is an arena for the ego's activity. Weak egos dissolve at death. Those that survive the shock of death gain, in the stage between death and resurrection, fresh opportunities for growth: Sufi experiences show that the ego, during this period, continues to possess consciousness. At its re-emergence, the ego's character manifests itself in the form of heaven or hell, which are states, not locations. But hell is not an eternal abode of misery, just as heaven is no holiday. The ego, in its new life after death and resurrection, continues to receive ever new opportunities for self-growth and creative self-unfolding.

5. 'The Spirit of Muslim Culture'

Both the prophet and the mystic have unitary experience. The mystic prefers to remain absorbed in the experience, and, if he at all returns from it, his return does not carry much significance for humankind at large. The prophet, on the other hand, always returns from the experience, determined to bring about a creative and constructive change in the world. A pragmatic test of the value of the prophet's religious experience would consist in examining the cultural world that the spirit of his message creates. This lecture looks at some of the ruling concepts of Islamic culture, aiming to comprehend the process of ideation underlying them. But, first, it is necessary to understand the importance, in Islam, of the idea of the finality of prophethood.

During the earlier stages of human evolution, psychic energy gives rise to prophetic consciousness, which, representing an economy of thought and action, provides ready-made judgements and solutions for the situations of life. This non-rational mode of consciousness is inhibited with the rise, at a later stage, of rational and critical faculties. Man is primarily ruled by passion and instinct. Inductive reason, which gives man control over the environment, is an achievement. The Prophet Muhammad stands at the junction of the ancient and modern worlds. The source of his message is ancient, but the spirit of his message is modern, for the birth of Islam is the birth of inductive intellect. With man having come of age intellectually, the doctrine of the finality of prophethood abolishes all supernaturally-sanctioned personal authority—whether religious or political. Thus, reason, experience, nature, and history, as sources of knowledge, assume special importance. The doctrine makes man rely on his own resources for the achievement of full consciousness. And while it regards mystic experience as natural, the doctrine subjects the knowledge yielded by this experience, like any other type of knowledge, to critical scrutiny. Finally, the doctrine renders superfluous the notion of messianic redemption, which, according to Oswald Spengler, is characteristic of the group of Magian religions—to which, Spengler mistakenly thinks, Islam belongs.

The Qur'anic view of nature as something concrete and its view of the universe as dynamic eventually led Muslim thinkers to revolt against the speculative Greek thought, which at first they had embraced. The revolt, joined by prominent theologians, philosophers, and scientists over a course of centuries, manifested itself in various branches of knowledge—in mathematics, astronomy, medicine, and logic. The experimental and inductive method, born of the anti-classical spirit of Islam, is the product of Islamic culture, from which it was borrowed by Europe.

Proportion was the Greek ideal; infinity is the Islamic. The notion of a dynamic universe that is capable of limitless growth finds expression in Islamic thought in several ways. The poet-thinker 'Iraqi postulates multiple space-orders and time-orders, rejecting the idea of an absolute time and an absolute space; the philosopher Ibn Miskawayh views life in terms of an evolutionary movement; and the philosophical historian Ibn Khaldun, taking his inspiration from the Qur'an, considers history to be a continuous and creative process of change.

6. 'The Principle of Movement in the Structure of Islam'

In Islam, the Ultimate Reality—God—is the eternal spiritual ground of all life, that expresses itself in variety and change. An Islamic society must, therefore, reconcile eternal principles with the possibilities of change, and it must have a principle of movement to mediate between the two categories. Ijtihad—technically, the endeavour to form an independent legal judgement—is such a principle in Islam. Our concern here is only with what is known as complete ijtihad—that is, ijtihad exercised at the foundational level.

The Sunnis, while theoretically allowing ijtihad, deny it in practice by making it almost impossible for a single individual to qualify for it. This strange intellectual attitude has immobilized the legal system of a religion whose scripture takes a dynamic view of life. The stagnation of Islamic law is due to the conservative Muslim thinkers' efforts to protect Islam's social fabric against the perceived disruptive effects of rationalistic views, to speculative

Sufism's indifference to Islam as a social polity, and to the jurists' protectionist banning of all innovation in the wake of the destruction of Baghdad in the thirteenth century.

The modern Turkish experiment in *ijtihad* is worth noting. The Nationalist Party accords primacy to the state as the institution that determines the functions of all other institutions, including religion. But Islam, instead of distinguishing between a religious domain and a temporal one, terms the same act spiritual or secular, depending on the mental attitude with which it is performed. Man is a unity, which, viewed as acting in relation to the external world, is body, but, viewed as acting in relation to the ultimate aim of such acting, is mind or soul. The state, from an Islamic standpoint, is only a medium for translating the ideal principles of *tawhid*, or oneness of God—equality, solidarity, and freedom—in a spatio-temporal context. Turkey's Religious Reform Party views Islam as a harmony of the ideal and the positive. It deplores the localization of the universal Islamic social and ethical ideals and calls upon Muslims to recover and reclaim those ideals. Turkey's Grand National Assembly has decreed that the caliphate may be vested in a group of persons or in an elected body. This *ijtihad* is consonant with the spirit of Islam and is also justified by the political realities of the modern Muslim world. The Turkish view of the Islamic international ideal is enunciated in the works of the poet-thinker Zia. The liberal movement in modern Islam is to be welcomed, but unchecked liberalism can become a force of disintegration.

Is the Law of Islam capable of evolution? The assimilative spirit of Islam will, under the right conditions, triumph over our scholars' legal conservatism. In the first few centuries of Islam, when the Qur'an was the only written law of Islam, Islam saw the rise of no fewer than nineteen legal schools. Muslim legal schools initially took a deductive, but later an increasingly inductive, approach to law. A review of the four major sources of Islamic law—Qur'an, *Hadith* (Prophetic Tradition), *ijma‘* (consensus), and *qiyas* (analogical reasoning)—will also explode the myth of the rigidity of our major legal schools, clearly suggesting at the same time the possibility of further evolution in the future. Keen thinking and fresh experience will enable Muslims to reconstruct Islamic systems. Political and economic developments on the world scene should awaken us to the inner meaning and destiny of Islam.

Today, humanity needs three things: a spiritual interpretation of the universe, spiritual liberation of the individual, and a set of basic principles of a universal character that would allow society to evolve on a spiritual basis. The idealistic systems that, employing pure reason, Europe has built on these lines lack the living conviction which personal revelation alone can generate. Muslims possess such a revelation. They believe in the spiritual basis of life, and the doctrine of the finality of prophethood liberates them from spiritual slavery. Muslims can, and should, work to achieve the ultimate goal of Islam—a spiritual democracy.

7. 'Is Religion Possible?'

Religious life passes through three phases—faith, thought, and discovery. As faith, religion is a discipline that demands unconditional submission. As thought, religion takes the form of a rational system, acquiring a metaphysics. In the phase of discovery, religious life aspires to a direct experience of the Ultimate Reality, with religious psychology displacing religious metaphysics. The word 'religion' in the title is used in this third sense. The term mysticism, used to describe the third and last phase of religious life, is unfortunate since mysticism is seen as life-negating and unempirical, whereas religion is essentially experience; religion, in fact, recognized the need to base itself on experience long before science did.

Kant's argument against the possibility of metaphysics applies equally to religion. But it assumes a distinction between the thing-in-itself—whose inaccessibility to reason makes rational demonstration of its existence impossible—and the-thing-as-it-appears-to-us. In view of recent developments in science, however, the case for rational theology is not so hopeless. The aforementioned Kantian dichotomy assumes that the so-called normal level of experience alone is capable of yielding knowledge, but other levels of experience, not amenable to conceptual analysis, may exist—as some Muslim thinkers have suggested.

One might object that levels of experience which cannot be conceptualized yield knowledge that is individual and incommunicable rather than universal in character. But the incommunicability of religious experience may reveal to us that religious life—whose essence is action or deed rather than thought or contemplation—culminates in the ego's acquisition, through contact with the Most Real, of a unique selfhood whose depths cannot be plumbed by concept. And deed, though it is individual and incommunicable, can also be socialized if it is employed by a group of people as a method of approaching the Real. The experiences of the world's religious experts give evidence of the existence of types of consciousness other than the normal type, and these types of consciousness, if they are life-giving and knowledge-yielding, are a legitimate subject of study. That such experiences are neurotic or mystical in character does not diminish their value or meaning. Modern psychology says that religion, instead of relating the human ego with an objective reality, serves only to inhibit the otherwise uncontrollable ego from disrupting society. This, however, is an elementary function of religion, whose real objective is to reconstitute the finite ego through contact with an eternal life-process.

There are also scientific and practical grounds for considering the question of non-normal—in this case, religious—experience. Modern mathematics and physics have already raised the question of whether nature is wholly explicable in terms of causation. And modern man, despite his immense control over the forces of nature, is living in a state of conflict with himself and with others and is experiencing life-weariness as a result. Religion alone affords a method of spiritual renewal that brings one into contact with the inexhaustible source of life and power.

Both religion and science aim at reaching the most real, the absolutely objective, and both seek to do so by critiquing experience and purifying it of subjective elements. Both religion and science deal with the same Reality—science with its observable behaviour, religion with its inner nature. The ego's standpoint is exclusive in the scientific process, inclusive in the religious. But the two processes are complementary, and the experience reached in both science and religion is equally natural.

B. Lectures: Exposition and Comment

We will now look at selected themes and motifs of the *Reconstruction*.

1. Theory of Knowledge

One of the main objectives of the *Reconstruction* is to establish religious experience as a valid source of knowledge. Iqbal is, of course, revisiting an old issue in Muslim intellectual history— or even in world intellectual history—the issue, namely, of the relationship between reason and revelation or, in modern terminology, science and religion. The main question can be stated thus: Is the knowledge gained through religious experience as reliable as the knowledge gained through—the so-called normal or objective—sensory experience? The main lines of Iqbal's argument—which answers the question in the affirmative—have been laid out above (see summaries of Lectures I, II, and VII). Nevertheless, a few observations are in order.

Iqbal tries to find a middle ground between—or rather, to synthesize—two concepts of knowledge-yielding experience, one scientific or Western and the other religious or Islamic. His attempt to do so is a good illustration of his declared aim in the book's Preface—namely, to reconstruct Muslim religious thought in the light of modern developments in knowledge. In the modern Western conception, knowledge is born of sensory experience; in the traditional, Sufi conception—in the Ghazalian formulation, for example—knowledge of the Ultimate Reality is gained through intuition. Iqbal accepts certain elements of each view while rejecting others. He accepts ordinary sense-perception as affording reliable knowledge and argues that the Qur'an, in opposition to the speculative thinkers of ancient Greece, takes an anti-classical—that is to say, empirical—view of the world in which we live, consequently treating the world as real. It was this 'general empirical attitude of the Qur'an which engendered in its followers a feeling of reverence for the actual and ultimately made them the founders of modern science' (I. 11). But Iqbal denies that knowledge arising out of sense-perception is the only type of knowledge available to human beings: he cites the fact that we know the existence of other minds not through sense perception but only inferentially (I. 13–4). Having thus made room for non-sensory knowledge, he posits—on the strength of the revealed and mystic literature's massive testimony—that intuition is a trustworthy medium of obtaining knowledge (I. 13; VII. 146, 149). 'The facts of religious experience', he concludes, 'are facts among other facts of human experience and, in the capacity of yielding knowledge by interpretation, one fact is as good as another' (I. 13). Intuitive knowledge, therefore, is no less objective and valid than ordinary sensory knowledge.

Iqbal's whole argument hinges on his particular understanding of the relationship between knowledge and experience. While granting that it is experience that produces knowledge, he broadens the base of experience to include in it religious experience. Knowledge, as long as it reflects authentic experience, is valid.

It is true that religious experience is, characteristically, in-communicable. But, according to Iqbal, the incommunicability of this experience 'does not mean that the religious man's pursuit is futile'. In fact, it

gives us a clue to the ultimate nature of the ego. . . . The climax of religious life, however, is the discovery of the ego as an individual deeper than his conceptually describable habitual self-hood. It is in contact with the Most Real that the ego discovers its uniqueness, its metaphysical status, and the possibility of improvement in that status. Strictly speaking, the experience which leads to this discovery is not a conceptually manageable intellectual fact; it is a vital fact, an attitude consequent on an inner biological transformation which cannot be captured in the net of logical categories. (VII. 145)

It is clear from this passage that Iqbal is at once legitimating religious experience as completely natural and distinguishing it from the ordinary or conscious experience of daily life. It is important to remember that Iqbal does not regard the two types of consciousness—ordinary and religious—as two perspectives on the same body of knowledge. Religion does not interpret the same data that science interprets; it 'aims at reaching the real significance of a special variety of human experience' (I. 20), 'The ultimate aim of religious life [being] the reconstruction of the finite ego by bringing him into contact with an eternal life process' (VII. 154).

To enlarge the scope of valid experience in order to include in it non-ordinary types of experience does not imply that all experience, no matter of what type, will always yield reliable knowledge. On the contrary, experience of every type—scientific or religious—is in need of interpretation or critical examination. A true mystic, like a true scientist, is always concerned with sifting the genuine elements of experience from the spurious, with a view to reaching the objective elements of experience and eliminating the subjective elements from it; Iqbal supports his claim by citing the views and methods of the sixteenth-century Indian Muslim mystic Ahmad Sirhindi (VII. 152–3; also 143–4). Nor is there anything 'irreverent' about critically examining religious experience (I. 13). In the *Reconstruction*, Iqbal himself applies, in Lectures II and V respectively, what he calls the intellectual and pragmatic tests to religious experience. The view that both the scientist and the mystic aim at the objectively real leads to what may be called the teleological harmony of science and religion:

The truth is that the religious and the scientific processes, though involving different methods, are identical in their final aim. Both aim at reaching the most real. In fact, religion, for reasons which I have mentioned before, is far more anxious to reach the ultimately real than science. And to both the way to pure objectivity lies through what may be called the purification of experience. (VII. 155)

By establishing the primacy of experience and, consequently, the naturalness of the non-rational as well as the rational mode of knowledge, Iqbal accomplishes the following:

(*a*) He (i) brings religion under the general rubric of validly obtained knowledge; (ii) highlights the distinctive nature of religion (knowledge obtained through religious experience, which is of the non-rational type—but no less reliable on that account); and (iii) underscores the need to interpret this knowledge and integrate it with other types of knowledge.

(*b*) He plausibly argues that science, which 'seeks to establish uniformities of experience, i.e. the laws of mechanical repetition' (II. 40), can effectively deal with only one of the three main levels of experience, that of matter—the other two levels being life and consciousness (II. 26). Religion, which 'demands the whole of Reality', need not be afraid of science (II. 34).

(*c*) He evaluates several individual theories in philosophy and science by applying to them the critical yardstick of experience. For example, he argues that Russell's attempt to solve Zeno's paradox by reference to Cantor's theory of mathematical continuity fails because 'The mathematical conception of continuity as infinite series applies not to movement regarded as an act, but rather to the picture of movement as viewed from the outside. The act of movement, i.e. movement as lived and not as thought, does not admit of any divisibility' (II. 30). Similarly, Einstein's Theory of Relativity, 'which deals only with the structure of things, throws no light on the ultimate nature of things which possess that structure' (II. 31). Moreover, the theory, by interpreting time to be a fourth dimension, denies the reality of time, neglecting 'certain characteristics of time as experienced by us' (II. 31).

In view of the above, one can say that a major contribution of Iqbal to Muslim thought consists in his attempt to break down the wall (erected by al-Ghazali) between analytic thought and religious consciousness. To this day, many Muslim intellectuals think that al-Ghazali won the day for Islam by positing a special— i.e. mystic—mode of consciousness that is distinct from the rational mode and is proof against rationalist doubt or attack. Iqbal rejects this idea by arguing, first, that religion itself is not without a strong rational element, and, second, that no watertight division between thought and intuition can be made. Al-Ghazali, it follows, took an unnecessarily restricted view of religion by choosing a non-rational basis for religion—a view that is 'not wholly justified by the spirit of the Qur'an' (I. 3).

It can be seen that Iqbal does not privilege any single approach to reality, but rather advocates using a multi-pronged—or rather, an integralist—approach to it, as when he says that sense-perception must be supplemented by intuition. Whether Iqbal himself succeeds in developing such an approach is not of central importance. The crucial thing is the method of inquiry proposed by him—a method that he derives from his study and understanding of the Islamic tradition taken in its broadest sense— and the promise that use of such a method holds for reaching a new synthesis of Islamic religious and intellectual tradition.

A concern is sometimes expressed about Iqbal's use of the word 'religious' in the key phrase 'religious experience'. How rigorous is he in using the word? Does he not, at times, somewhat carelessly employ the words 'religious', 'mystic', 'prophetic', and 'psychic' interchangeably? This question will be taken up later in this chapter.

2. Time

Iqbal gives considerable attention to the problem of time. The problem is important, in the first place, because time implies history and change. According to some writers, religions fall into three categories: religions of nature, which focus on the cyclical or recurring patterns of nature, consequently denying reality to historical time; religions of contemplation, which seek salvation in an enduring world of changeless spirit as contrasted with a transient world of changeful matter, and, in doing so, deny that historical time is real; and religions of history, which take the past, present, and future to be distinct but connected categories of thought and action, and view human salvation working itself out through historical time. From Iqbal's perspective, Islam would pre-eminently qualify as a religion of history. Time represents an affirmation of history, which represents, in turn, an affirmation of the principle of change—and, by clear implication, an acceptance of the inexorable law of life that societies' survival and progress depend on their making a resourceful and effective response to constantly changing circumstances. This response includes the strategies not only of adaptation and adjustment to change but also of anticipation, appropriation, and control of change. We can already see how this view of time, with its declaration of the reality of the material world, its recommendation and approbation of taking an empirical approach to that world, with its prescription of action as necessary to success, and with its implied promise of human mastery over the forces of life and nature, fits in with Iqbal's overall world-view and with his philosophy of *khudi* or self-affirmation (see Chapter 2).

But the issue of time is important for other reasons as well. While Iqbal regards historical time as real, he does not think that historicity exhausts the reality of time. He distinguishes between pure time and serial time. Serial time is 'the time of which we predicate long and short'; it is time divided into the categories of past, present, and future. Time thus conceived is a useful tool employed by the efficient self or 'the practical self of daily life in its dealing with the external order of things' (II. 38). Being 'the essence of causality as defined by Kant' (II. 31), it is 'hardly distinguishable from space, but 'beneath the appearance of serial duration there is true duration' (II. 48), which is change without succession' (II. 46). This is time as experienced from the inside—by the appreciative self rather than the efficient self: it is 'time as felt and not as thought or calculated' (II. 40; also 38–9). Serial time comes into existence because the Ultimate Reality or the Divine Self, which 'exists in pure duration' (II. 48), in the process of its becoming or self-unfolding, 'exposes its ceaseless creative activity to quantitative measurement' (II. 46–7).

Though serial time and pure duration are distinct from each other, they are not unrelated. In distinguishing between the two, Iqbal uses expressions like 'standpoint' and 'point of view', indicating that the distinction is not a dichotomy. Serial time, in the end, is 'organically related to eternity in the sense that it is a measure of non-successional change' (III. 61).

Iqbal's concept of time, with its distinction between serial time and pure time, has several theoretical and practical implications. To begin with, by first distinguishing between, and then integrating, the two, Iqbal is able to argue that thought (which deals with Reality piecemeal—that is, in serial time) and intuition (which apprehends Reality as a whole—that is, in pure duration), too, are organically related (I. 2, 5). This relationship between thought and intuition obviates the need to posit a non-rational basis for religion—and this reinforces Iqbal's critique of al-Ghazali's rejection of analytic reason as a basis for religion (see above). Furthermore, the vision that our reflective contact with temporality affords us is not merely of intellectual value, but is—under the right circumstances—creative of new possibilities of action in the material world. For just as the Ultimate Reality's non-temporal creativity is translated into quantifiable units of historical time, so man, having experienced pure duration through the appreciative self's agency, creates new possibilities of action within the framework of serial time on his return from that experience. Equipped with the perspective of the non-temporal, man is able to manipulate the temporal—as if, standing at an extraterrestrial point, he were able to manipulate the earth with an Archimedean lever. The tremendous energy unleashed by the prophetic personalities is explained by the ability of the prophets to translate creatively their vision of the non-temporal into concrete modes of thought and action in historical contexts. It is on account of the similarity between the potential creativity of man with the creativity of the Ultimate Reality that Iqbal, in more than one place, calls man God's co-worker.

The distinction between serial time and pure time also helps us to understand the important concept of *taqdir* or destiny: misunderstood as fixed, determinate future (and called *kismet*), it has had a numbing effect on Muslim thought and action in history. Iqbal remarks:

> Pure time, then, as revealed by a deeper analysis of our conscious experience, is not a string of separate, reversible instants; it is an organic whole in which the past is not left behind, but is moving along with, and operating in, the present. And the future is given to it not as lying before, yet to be traversed; it is given only in the sense that it is present in its nature as an open possibility. . . . Destiny is time regarded as prior to the disclosure of its possibilities. It is time freed from the net of causal sequence—the diagrammatic character which the logical understanding imposes upon it. In one word, it is time as felt and not as thought and calculated. . . . Time regarded as destiny forms the very essence of things. (II. 39–40)

The key phrase in this quote is 'the future . . . as an open possibility'—and this phrase sums up Iqbal's view of *taqdir*. To Iqbal, therefore, *taqdir*—'which has been so much misunderstood both in and outside Islam' (I. 40)—is a dynamic concept that ought to encourage and promote, rather than discourage and kill, creative thought and action.

It is often alleged that Iqbal borrows his concept of time from the French philosopher Henri Bergson. Iqbal has certainly been influenced by Bergson, and his own writings testify to the influence. But there are some crucial differences between the views of Bergson and Iqbal. For example, both Bergson and Iqbal take pure time to be a free creative movement. But while

Bergson understands this movement to be non-teleological—since teleology, to him, makes time unreal—Iqbal takes that movement to be teleological, though, in explaining his view of teleology, he distinguishes between purpose and destination (II. 43–4; see also Iqbal's view of *taqdir*, above). Iqbal writes:

The world-process, or the movement of the universe in time, is certainly devoid of purpose, if by purpose we mean a foreseen end—a far-off destination to which the whole creation moves. To endow the world-process with purpose in this sense is to rob it of its originality and its creative character. Its ends are terminations of a career; they are ends to come and not necessarily terminated. A time-process cannot be conceived as a line already drawn. It is a line in the drawing— an actualisation of open possibilities. . . . To my mind nothing is more alien to the Qur'anic outlook than the idea that the universe is a temporal working out of a preconceived plan. (II. 44)

Furthermore, unlike Bergson, Iqbal predicates pure time of a self:

I venture to think that the error of Bergson consists in regarding pure time as prior to self to which alone pure duration is predicable. Neither pure space nor pure time can hold together the multiplicity of objects and events. It is the appreciative act of an enduring self only which can seize the multiplicity of duration—broken up into an infinity of instants—and transform it to the organic wholeness of a synthesis. (II. 44–5)

Finally, Iqbal speaks approvingly of the Sufi poet-thinker 'Iraqi's concept of multiple time-orders. 'Iraqi's distinction between the serial time of gross bodies and immaterial beings and the non-serial time of the Divine Being (III. 60–1) is not likely to find favour with Bergson: in 'Iraqi's view, Divine time, as Iqbal puts it, 'is absolutely free from the quality of passage, and consequently does not admit of divisibility, sequence, and change. It is above eternity; it has neither beginning nor end' (III. 60). In other words, God is prior to time (III. 60)—a conclusion that would be unacceptable to Bergson. It would seem that, while Iqbal borrows certain elements of thought from Muslim and non-Muslim thinkers, the overall structure of the concept of time he presents is his own.

It cannot, of course, be maintained that Iqbal has solved all the issues pertaining to the philosophy of time. Several elements in Iqbal's thesis are unclear. For example, Iqbal says that God exists in pure time but that the appreciative self of man, too, can, under certain conditions, participate in pure time. Is there, one might ask, any qualitative difference between God's being in pure time and man's being in pure time? Iqbal also maintains that pure time's movement is purposive but not destination-bound. But how can one conceive of purposiveness in disjunction from a definite or specific goal? And one even wonders whether vindication of the claim about the absolute freedom of pure time's movement will not require the elimination of all purpose from the scheme of things. It should be remembered, however, that Iqbal's concept of time, besides being an exercise in philosophy, serves a practical purpose as well. It affirms the possibility of a developed human ego stepping outside the rigid scheme of mechanistic causation and becoming creative in the temporal world through contact with, or experience of, the non-temporal.

3. God, Nature, and Man

To call God a self is to say that God is a personality and not an abstraction or a principle. God is a self in an absolute sense; man is a self in a contingent sense; and nature is the not-self (see summary of Lecture II, above). According to this statement, both man and nature are dependent upon God, who is their creator and sustainer. But the statement also implies that, in respect of selfhood, man stands between God and nature. Man's position, however, is not 'equidistant' from God and nature; he does not represent, so to speak, a mean between God and nature. Nor is He to be conceived as a mediator between God (whose Absolute Self will not be enhanced by mediation) and nature (whose not-self will not gain in status from any mediation). Between God as a stable reference point and nature as a static one, man alone is the great variable, and his true status in the chain of being will be determined by his conduct. His mandate from God is the harnessing of the forces of nature for wholesome purposes, knowledge of which he acquires from God, the source of all value. Man, then, is a Janus-like creature: his efficient self enables him to deal with nature, which exists in serial time—limiting and constraining his action. But his appreciative self enables him to experience pure time, which is the time of God—the source of all creativity. Experience of pure time thus equips man with creative freedom, which he can use to create new opportunities of action in the arena of nature. This point is brought out, in a slightly different context, by the following quote from the *Reconstruction*:

Man . . . occupies a genuine place in the heart of Divine creative energy and thus possesses a much higher degree of reality than things around him. Of all the creations of God he alone is capable of consciously participating in the creative life of his Maker. Endowed with the power to imagine a better world, and to mould what is into what ought to be, the ego in him aspires, in the interests of an increasingly unique and comprehensive individuality, to exploit all the various environments on which he may be called upon to operate during the course of an endless career. (III. 58)

The words 'endless career' in this quote deserve attention. Iqbal, in conformity with the standard Islamic doctrine, believes that death does not mean total extinction for man. Furthermore, man, who 'in his inmost being . . . is a creative activity, an ascending spirit' (I. 10), continues to evolve after death (see summary of Lecture IV, above). Iqbal also seems to think that survival after death is not to be taken for granted. While man is destined to be immortal, immortality 'is not ours as of right; it is to be achieved by personal effort. Man is only a candidate for it' (IV. 95).

Iqbal calls nature God's habit or character. His view of the relationship between God and nature ostensibly makes him an immanentist. Does he, then, deny God's transcendence? Not necessarily. Iqbal does not see a contradiction between Divine transcendence and immanence. Several indications in the *Reconstruction* lead one to that conclusion. First, we have already noted that, according to Iqbal, while knowledge of nature can be acquired through reflective observation on nature, God is known by intuition; Iqbal quotes with approval Ibn 'Arabi's dictum that 'God is a percept, the world is a concept' (VII. 144). Second, God is infinite, but His infinity, unlike that of nature, is intensive rather than spatial in character (III. 52), which clearly implies that God's immanence is not necessarily exclusive of His transcendence. Third, strictly speaking, what is revealed in nature is the symbols, not the person, of God, who, therefore, can also be said to transcend nature since nature *points* to Him.

In the early stages of his intellectual career, Iqbal was inclined towards a pantheistic view of existence. Later, however, he rejected the view and came to hold that man's destiny was not to lose himself in the person of God, but to preserve his individuality even when he had achieved—and this is the most he can achieve—proximity to God. 'In the higher Sufism of Islam unitive experience is not the finite ego effacing its own identity by some sort of absorption into the Infinite Ego; it is rather the Infinite passing into the loving embrace of the finite' (IV. 88). In this connection, it may be pointed out that Iqbal's interpretation of Hallaj's statement, 'I am the creative truth', is highly original and one that may well be the most satisfying explanation of those famous—and controversial—words.

4. *Ijtihad*

Lecture VI, 'The Principle of Movement in the Structure of Islam', underscores the need to reconstruct Islamic law (see summary of the lecture, above). A treatment of Iqbal's views on Islamic law would properly seem to belong to Chapter 5, but it is being offered here for three reasons. First, it will round off our treatment here of some of the salient ideas of the *Reconstruction*. Second, it will bring home the important fact that Iqbal's views on law are grounded in a certain philosophical outlook. Third, it will illustrate a still more important fact—namely, that Iqbal's philosophy—and that includes his metaphysics—is not offered in isolation from, but has a direct bearing on, the world of practical reality.

The 'principle' referred to in the title of the lecture is *ijtihad*, which is commonly translated as 'independent reasoning', but which signifies responsible intellectual effort exerted to arrive at a legal ruling on a matter that is not clearly pronounced upon in the fundamental sources of Islamic law, namely, the Qur'an and the *Sunnah* (Prophetic Exemplary Conduct, as recorded in Hadith). Iqbal's description of *ijtihad* as a principle of movement is significant, since it highlights the importance *ijtihad* has, in Iqbal's view, in the scheme of Islamic intellectual and social life. We have seen that Iqbal's world-view is dynamic—according to him, change and movement characterize all existence. It is in the context of this general philosophical conception of the dynamic nature of the universe and of human life that Iqbal states his views on Islamic law. Society, like everything else, undergoes constant change—and, consequently, has to reckon with the demands of change. But unbridled change is no less a destructive force than blind rigidity. *Ijtihad*, accordingly, is the Islamic instrument for accommodating and negotiating change in society. It goes without saying that *ijtihad* must be carried out within the limits proper to it.

We can appreciate the urgency of Iqbal's case for *ijtihad* if we remember that, in Sunni legal theory at least, the door of *ijtihad* had—if not theoretically then practically—been closed for many centuries. Thus, in stressing the need for *ijtihad*, Iqbal was challenging a highly entrenched religious conservatism. For his times, Iqbal made a rather daring statement when, in approving of certain political developments that were taking place in Turkey, he remarked that, from an Islamic standpoint, rulership of a Muslim society may be vested in a corporate body like an elected assembly (VI. 124). Iqbal is cautious not to give unqualified approval to the Turkish experiment in political and social matters, and he expresses grave reservations about certain aspects of the new Turkish programme of reform. In principle, however, Iqbal would allow a reinterpretation of even the 'foundational legal principles' of Islam in the light of Muslims' experience in modern times (VI. 134). What, in his view, is crucial for Muslims to guard and preserve is 'the ultimate aims of Islam as a social polity' (VI. 134), and these ultimate aims he identifies, following the medieval Muslim jurist Abu Ishaq al-Shatibi (d. 1388), as 'the five general things—Din (Religion), Nafs (Life), 'Aql (Reason), Mal (Property), and Nasl (Progeny)' (VI. 134). The advice to Muslim legists to have recourse to these five supreme objectives amounts to a plea for a complete recodification of Islamic law. Iqbal is not the first Muslim modernist to argue for the objectives-based approach to Islamic law: others, notably Rashid Rida of Syria (d. 1935), spoke highly of Shatibi and his approach, and Iqbal may have been influenced by Rashid Rida's views. In the Indian subcontinent at least, Iqbal seems to be the first Muslim writer to have stressed the importance of doing what may be called basic research in Islamic law. It is probably distinctive of Iqbal in the history of modern Islamic reform that he not only wants to revisit Islamic law from a juristic standpoint, but is also quite willing to consider a modern Muslim country's experiments in law a source of legal insight, even when such a country—like the self-declared secular state of Turkey—were to make a significant departure from traditionally established sanctions and practices of Islamic law. Also, Iqbal belongs to a very small group of modern Muslim thinkers who have faith in the common people's ability to contribute to the revivification of Islamic religious thought. His views on ijma' are a case in point:

The transfer of the power of Ijtihad from individual representatives of schools to a Muslim legislative assembly which, in view of the growth of opposing sects, is the only possible form Ijma' can take in modern times, will secure contributions to legal discussion from laymen who happen to possess a keen insight into affairs. In this way alone we can stir into activity the dormant spirit of life in our legal system, and give it an evolutionary outlook. (VI. 138)

'The Principle of Movement in the Structure of Islam' is, simultaneously, a bold affirmation of faith in the ability of Islamic law to evolve with changing circumstances and a passionate plea for the restoration of 'the inner catholicity of the spirit of Islam' in modern times (VI. 131). Many regard this to be the finest lecture in the *Reconstruction*.

5. Islamic Doctrines as Operating Principles in Society

Convinced that Islam as a religion can succeed only if it brings into existence a viable polity, Iqbal constantly tries to discover the intellectual and social meanings and implications of Islamic doctrines. Consider, for example, *tawhid*, the most fundamental article of faith in Islam. 'Islam, as a polity', Iqbal says, 'is only a practical means of making this principle a living factor in the intellectual and emotional life of mankind' (VI. 117). Thus, Islam 'rejects blood-relationship as a basis of human unity' (VI. 116) and seeks to unite humanity on the basis of the psychological or spiritual principle of *tawhid*, for it 'demands loyalty to God, not to thrones' (VI. 117). We spoke above of the importance of *ijtihad* in Iqbal's thought. Iqbal derives what we may call the *ijtihad* imperative direct from *tawhid*. God is 'the ultimate spiritual basis of all life', which is 'eternal and reveals itself in variety and change'. So, a society that holds to *tawhid* 'must reconcile, in its life, the categories of permanence and change', *ijtihad* being the principle that enables Muslim society to reconcile Islam's eternal principles with the demands of change (VI. 117).

A word may also be said about the Islamic concept of the finality of prophethood as understood by Iqbal (see summary of Lecture V, above). On the one hand, this concept served to pave the way for the rise of the inductive method—whose discovery was one of the principal contributions Muslims made to world civilization. But the concept also imparts an existential character to the human situation on earth: from now on, man must rely on himself for his salvation. Pushed to its logical conclusion, the concept may even be said to announce the end of the age of miracles and usher in the age of scientific causation. A thoroughly religious concept thus becomes the cornerstone of rational attitude in the field of knowledge, and of egalitarian polity in the field of conduct.

We will conclude this chapter with a few general remarks about the *Reconstruction*.

First, the *Reconstruction* is a testimony to the author's erudition and critical acumen. In this book, Iqbal discusses, cites, or refers to the works and ideas of over one hundred and fifty thinkers and writers belonging to the vast Islamic and Western philosophical and literary traditions, including theologians, legists, philosophers, scientists, historians, mystics, and poets—both of classical and modern periods. Iqbal presents summaries, along with his critical comments, of the theories or views of many of these authorities. Examples of such treatments are the Muslim theologians' atomistic theories (III. 54–7), Abu Hanifa's view of the Prophetic traditions of a legal character (VI. 136–7), Bergson's vitalism (II. 37–8, 41–4), Einstein's Theory of Relativity (II. 30–1), Spengler's theory of culture (V. 114–15), 'Iraqi's concept of multiple time-orders and space-orders (III. 60–1; V. 107–8; VII. 144), and Rumi's verses that have epistemological significance (III. 72–3). Iqbal makes some highly interesting and suggestive comparisons between Muslim and Western writers. For example, he notes that 'Ghazali's mission was almost apostolic like that of Kant in Germany', both philosophers successfully challenging the proud rationalism of their respective ages (I. 4); that Ibn Rushd's concept of immortality 'looks like William James's suggestion of a transcendental mechanism of consciousness which operates on a physical medium for a while, and then gives it up in pure sport' (IV. 89); and that 'Iraqi's concept of 'the interpenetration of the super-spatial "here" and super-eternal "now" in the Ultimate Reality suggests the modern notion of space-time which Professor [Samuel] Alexander, in his lectures on "Space, Time, and Deity", regards as the matrix of all things' (V. 109). Iqbal points out what he thinks are crucial omissions in historical Islamic thought. For example, he remarks that, in view of the Qur'anic emphasis on the 'individuality and uniqueness of man, . . . it is surprising to see that the unity of human consciousness which constitutes the centre of human personality never really became a point of interest in the history of Muslim thought' (IV. 77). Furthermore, he notes and evaluates the divergent or conflicting currents of thought within the Western intellectual tradition. For example, he observes that Nietzsche's doctrine of eternal recurrence, in granting the possibility of immortality, constitutes a significant exception to modern materialism's rejection of immortality (IV. 91–2), and remarks that 'Whitehead's view of Relativity is likely to appeal to Muslim students more than Einstein's' (V. 106). Finally, on several occasions, Iqbal points out the direction in which the task of the reconstruction of Muslim thought in modern times must proceed. For example, he stresses the need to study classical Islamic theological thought in the light of modern physics (III. 54–5). Iqbal has been called an original thinker, and the *Reconstruction* offers justification for that view. As noted above, the *Reconstruction* treats the thoughts and ideas of numerous thinkers and writers from diverse backgrounds. Everywhere, however, these thoughts and ideas are harnessed into the service of Iqbal's own intellectual project, and nowhere do they dominate or overpower that project. Iqbal draws the elements of his own philosophy from various sources, but—through critique, adaptation, and reinterpretation—he integrates them into a framework of thought that is unmistakably his own.

Second, a careful reading of the *Reconstruction* will show that, in a certain definite sense, Iqbal can be called a systematic thinker. The *Reconstruction* is a difficult work, and certain peculiarities of Iqbal's style and presentation can create the impression that Iqbal does not offer a sustained treatment of the issues he raises. At times, allusive brevity and extended digression make it difficult to follow the line of argument. Nevertheless, taken as a whole, the work has a well-defined scope and a set of clearly stated themes. Introducing the subject-matter of the first lecture, Iqbal writes: 'I propose, in this preliminary lecture, to consider the character of knowledge and religious experience' (I. 7). The opening lecture does, in fact, serve as an outline for much of the book, and most of the remaining lectures elucidate the themes that are explicitly or implicitly stated in the first. Throughout the book, Iqbal focuses on these themes, frequently referring the reader to his discussion of them in other parts of the book, and seldom, if ever, departing from those themes. For instance, the concepts of the Ultimate Reality, experience, and time are discussed from various angles in several lectures. Such concepts, taken together, constitute the bedrock of Iqbal's philosophical argument in the book. Furthermore, the treatment of several of the themes in the individual lectures is clear and cogent. As an example that is relatively easy to follow, but is nonetheless representative, one can cite the third lecture, 'The Conception of God and the Meaning of Prayer' (see summary above). Finally, the seven lectures are closely interlinked, as a study of their contents will show. For example, at the end of the first lecture, Iqbal speaks of two tests of religious experience, one intellectual and one pragmatic. The second lecture ('The Philosophical Test of the Revelations of Religious Experience') applies the intellectual test to religious experience, while the fifth lecture ('The Spirit of Muslim Culture') applies the pragmatic test. Similarly, the discussion of the Absolute Ego in the third lecture logically leads to the discussion of the human ego in the fourth ('The Human Ego—His Freedom and Immortality'). It is my impression that the *Reconstruction*, in its entirety, represents the detailed working out of a single master idea, tersely expressed by Iqbal in the phrase 'the immanent Infinite' (I. 5). A separate study is needed to elucidate the matter, however. Meanwhile, the view that Iqbal is a systematic thinker does not imply that Iqbal's thought has no weak points or is completely free from contradiction, or is not subject to the charge of lack of coherence. All that is being maintained is that—whatever lacunae and shortcomings it may have—the thought-content of the book has an essential unity of structure, and that—whatever weaknesses it may appear to have—the method employed in the work has an essential self-consistency.

Third, a reader of the *Reconstruction* cannot but be struck by the centrality of the Qur'an to Iqbal's thought. All Muslim thinkers—whether theologians, legists, philosophers, or others—appeal to the Qur'an as the ultimate sanction for their thought, even though they may differ in their approach to and interpretation of the Qur'an. Thus, there exists a tradition of Islamic philosophical interpretation of the Qur'an. Iqbal may be said to belong to that tradition, but he would seem to occupy a unique position in it. Unlike some of the other Muslim philosophers, who use Qur'anic verses as pegs on which to hang ideas that have little or nothing to do with the letter or spirit of the Qur'an, Iqbal draws his fundamental inspiration from the Qur'an. For example, his treatment of the Islamic view of man and the universe (Lecture I) and of the conception of God (Lecture III) is firmly grounded in the Qur'an. At the same time, Iqbal offers a series of insights that are as fresh as they are startling. To take one or two examples: Iqbal sees a clear connection between the Qur'anic emphasis on man's individuality and the Qur'anic views on personal accountability and vicarious salvation: 'It is in consequence of this view of man as a unique individuality which makes it impossible for one individual to bear the burden of another, and entitles him only to what is due to his personal effort, that the Qur'an is led to reject the idea of redemption' (IV. 76). He argues that, in its treatment of the story of Adam, the Qur'an uses the name 'Adam' as a concept rather than as a proper name, citing in his support Qur'an 7. 11, in which human beings are first addressed as a collectivity and then called Adam—as if they were a single individual. The verse reads: 'We created you; then fashioned you; then said We to the angels, "prostrate yourself unto Adam".' It is true that Iqbal has been criticized for his interpretations of the Qur'an, many of which have been termed unconvincing. Such judgements are probably a little hasty and seem to have been passed without due regard to the distinctive character of philosophical exegesis: one could pass similar judgements about the so-called legal, theological, or mystical interpretations of the Qur'an. Iqbal's philosophical exegesis, moreover, is probably *sui generis* (see Chapter 2, Section VII, for examples). It needs to be studied in its own right, and the principles from which it proceeds need to be grasped from Iqbal's own writings. The Qur'anic interpretations of a man who consciously took the Qur'an to be the most important source of spiritual and intellectual guidance in his personal life, who spent the better part of his life reflecting on the major issues of life in the light of the Qur'an, and who cited the Qur'an with great facility in his writings, should at least be regarded as plausible and deserving of close and careful study before being rejected. The failure to appreciate Iqbal's approach to the Qur'an is, in fact, part of the larger neglect from which Iqbal's serious thought—especially that expressed in his prose writings—has suffered.

Fourth, the lectures were written for delivery either before an Indian audience with a Western-style education (the first six lectures) or before a Western audience (the seventh). Keeping this fact in mind will help the reader to understand the language and idiom Iqbal uses to express himself; it will, especially, dispel some misgivings that might arise in the minds of some Muslim readers. Sometimes, Iqbal himself seems to anticipate such misgivings and, accordingly, offers what amounts to a clarification. For example, the second sentence in the following passage seems to be a footnote to the first: 'The world-life intuitively sees its own needs, and at critical moments defines its own direction. This is what, in the language of religion, we call prophetic religion' (VI. 117). A traditionally minded Muslim audience might interpret a 'world-life [that] intuitively see its own needs and defines its own direction' to be a self-directed impersonal force that either negates the existence of a personal deity or works independently of such a deity, whereas Iqbal's concern simply is to bridge the gap between traditional Islamic language and modern philosophical idiom. Sometimes, however, one wonders whether Iqbal uses some of his key terms with sufficient logical rigour. For example, one might ask what he means by 'religious experience', for he seems frequently to use religious experience synonymously with mystic—and occasionally with psychic—experience, and one suspects that he either treats all of these phrases on a par with one another or fails to distinguish between them properly. A closer study of the matter leads to a different conclusion, however. In the domain of knowledge, Iqbal is mainly interested in distinguishing between rational and non-rational knowledge. Prophetic, mystic, and psychic knowledge fall into the larger category of non-rational, or intuitive, knowledge. It is the common distinction of these three types of knowledge from rational knowledge that is of prime importance in Iqbal's scheme, and Iqbal's stress on their distinction from rational knowledge may create the impression that the three types, when taken by themselves, are held by Iqbal to be either identical or very similar to one another. But while they may resemble one another in some ways, and may even overlap in some areas, the three types of knowledge are distinguished from one another by Iqbal. His following statement, for example, underscores a crucial difference between religion and mysticism: 'The mystic's condemnation of knowledge as an organ of knowledge does not really find any justification in the history of religion' (I. 17–8). Iqbal also remarks that the act of worship is, in the case of prophetic consciousness, 'creative' (III. 71), whereas in the case of mystic consciousness it is 'cognitive' (III. 71). Both the prophet and the mystic return from the experience of intimacy with the eternal, but the prophet's return, unlike the mystic's, 'may be fraught with infinite meaning for mankind' (I. 18; see V. 99). In another context, Iqbal criticizes Duncan Black MacDonald for failing to differentiate between prophetic and psychic knowledge (I. 14). Iqbal's main thrust, in other words, is to establish the credentials of so-called non-rational knowledge. If this can be accomplished, it would be perfectly legitimate to engage in a 'scientific' discourse about religion, and other issues, such as the distinction of revealed from mystic or psychic knowledge, could be sorted out with greater precision later. Finally, we may need to remind ourselves that the audience of the lectures was more conversant with Western than with Islamic thought, and, in Western parlance, prophetic, mystic, and psychic knowledge are frequently labelled or associated with religious knowledge. Iqbal sought to make his views accessible to his audience without taking serious issue with this understanding—for that would have taken him too far-afield—but, at the same time, without necessarily granting the validity of that understanding.

Fifth, the *Reconstruction* evinces Iqbal's strong faith in the possibility of Islam's rejuvenation in the modern period. Iqbal is convinced that 'the Islamic renaissance is a fact' (VI. 121). But, in his view, this renaissance must fulfil certain conditions in order to become a full-fledged movement of growth and progress, one of the most important conditions being intellectual openness. Iqbal stresses that the West owes a great deal—above all, its scientific outlook and scientific method—to Islam (V. 103–4). At the same time, Iqbal unhesitatingly admits that it is now the Muslims' turn to learn from the West. Noting the speed with which 'the world of Islam is spiritually moving towards the West', he says: 'There is nothing wrong in this movement, for European culture, on its intellectual side, is only a further development of some of the most important phases of the culture of Islam' (I. 6). His worry, though, is that Muslims will be too dazzled by the exterior of European culture to 'reach the true inwardness of that culture' (I. 6). And so, he advises Muslims 'to examine, in an independent spirit, what Europe has thought and how far the conclusions reached by her can help us in the revision and, if necessary, reconstruction, of theological thought in Islam' (I. 6). Iqbal is concerned mainly with the task of reconstruction of Islamic thought; to this end, not only the Islamic but also the non-Islamic intellectual and cultural legacy is grist to his mill. The Preface to the *Reconstruction* concludes with the words, 'Our duty is carefully to watch the progress of human thought, and to maintain an independent attitude towards it' (p. xxii). But intellectual openness demands, above all, that Muslims be willing to re-examine their own heritage with a critical eye. In this connection, Iqbal cites Turkey. While he does not give blanket approval to the modernist thought of Turkey, Iqbal does say that, 'among the Muslim nations of to-day, Turkey alone has shaken off its dogmatic slumber, and attained to self-consciousness. She alone has claimed her right of intellectual freedom; she alone has passed from the ideal to the real' (VI. 108). The modern Turk, Iqbal says, is inspired 'by the realities of experience, and not by the scholastic reasoning of jurists who lived and thought under different conditions of life' (VI. 125–6). He suspects, or rather hopes, that 'we [Muslims of India] too one day, like the Turks, will have to re-evaluate our intellectual inheritance' (VI. 121). While deploring the conservatism of the Muslim masses (VI. 131), Iqbal encourages Muslim scholars to rekindle the spirit of free, but responsible, inquiry. In several places in the book, he points out the direction that the project of the reconstruction of Islamic thought should take (for example, III. 55–6, 58).

III. METAPHYSICS AND RECONSTRUCTION COMPARED

The *Metaphysics* and the *Reconstruction* may be compared in the following terms:

1. Common Elements

Although the *Metaphysics* and *Reconstruction* differ in purpose, scope, and approach, they are similar in some respects. Both works are of a high scholarly calibre. In both, Iqbal draws on a wide range of Eastern and Western sources of learning. Annemarie Schimmel in *Gabriel's Wing* speaks of Iqbal's 'unique way of weaving a grand tapestry of thought from eastern and western yarns' (p. xv). This skill of Iqbal's, while at its most impressive in the *Reconstruction*, is already evident in the *Metaphysics*.

The two works reveal certain basic philosophical preoccupations of Iqbal. In the *Metaphysics*, Iqbal limits himself to an investigation of 'the sacred trinity of philosophy—God, Man and Nature' (p. 4), and this, essentially, is the scope of the *Reconstruction* as well.

Certain categories of thought and analysis seem to be common to both works. A case in point is Iqbal's use of the categories of 'Semitic' and 'Aryan', coined by Western scholarship to distinguish the passionate, emotive, and action-oriented Semitic from the sober, rational, and idea-oriented Aryan. In the *Metaphysics* Iqbal remarks that Aryan Persia converted Semitic Islam to its own 'habits of thought', just as the Aryan Hellenic intellect had 'interpreted another Semitic religion—Christianity' (p. 21).

Elsewhere in the same book, he says that the enduring thought and practice of Sufism is due to 'Sufism's successful synthesization of the Semitic and Aryan tendencies' (p. 83). In the *Reconstruction* he observes that the criticism by the legists Malik and Shafi'i of Abu Hanifa's legal principle of Analogy 'constitutes really an effective Semitic restraint on the Aryan tendency to seize the abstract in preference to the concrete, to enjoy the idea rather than the event' (VI. 140). Another example of 'categorical' ideas is Iqbal's view that the genius of the Arab race was practical. This view becomes the basis of certain judgements and evaluations in Iqbal. In the *Metaphysics*, Iqbal says that 'the Arab genius was thoroughly practical; hence Plato's philosophy would have been distasteful to them even if it had been presented in its true light' (p. 136). In the *Reconstruction*, he observes that 'The legists of Hijaz, however, true to the practical genius of their race, raised strong protests against the scholastic subtleties of the legists of Iraq' (p. 140). The presence of such categories of thought and analysis in Iqbal's works indicates that some of his ideas—whether borrowed or not—had been formed quite early and were used by him at various stages of his intellectual career.

2. Differences

Clearly evidenced in both the *Metaphysics* and the *Reconstruction*, Iqbal's historical erudition becomes ancillary to the latter work's predominantly critical and constructive approach. The *Metaphysics* uses a diachronic approach, treating developments in Persian metaphysical thought in historical sequence. The *Reconstruction* employs a synchronic approach, the discussion throughout the book revolving around a set of interconnected issues. The *Metaphysics* aims at presenting a systematic account of certain aspects of Persian philosophical thought from pre-Islamic to modern times. The *Reconstruction*, conceived on a much more ambitious scale, seeks to restructure Islamic religious thought in the light of a critical understanding of modern—that is, Western—thought.

The two works differ in respect of the position of Qur'anic thought in them. The few references to the Qur'an in the

Metaphysics are either incidental or general in nature. In the *Reconstruction*, the number of Qur'anic citations have multiplied, but, more important, the Qur'an supplies the warp and woof of the book's thought and argument.

The first six lectures of the *Reconstruction* were published twenty years after the appearance of the *Metaphysics*. During this period, Iqbal's thought not only gained in breadth and depth, but it also underwent, it seems, a qualitative change and a significant reorientation. For example, Iqbal's attitude towards Sufism differs markedly from the one book to the other. In the *Metaphysics*, the longest chapter—the fifth—is devoted to Sufism, and Iqbal, who ascribes an Islamic foundation to Sufism and contrasts Sufism with Islamic law (to the latter's disadvantage), is obviously sympathetic to Sufism—to pantheistic Sufism, one might say. In the *Reconstruction*, on the contrary, Iqbal warns against the excesses of a pantheistic spiritual doctrine and praises Sufis who sought to purge Muslim mysticism of decadent elements. In this book, furthermore, he accords an important position to Islamic law in his overall scheme for the reform of Islamic thought and discusses at length the concept of *ijtihad*, the principle of movement in Islam.

An interesting example of how Iqbal came to change or modify his views from the *Metaphysics* to the *Reconstruction* is afforded by a certain passage of Rumi he quotes in translation in both works (*Metaphysics*, 91; *Reconstruction*, IV. 97). The passage purports to talk about evolution, describing how inorganic matter, passing through the vegetative and animal states, finally reaches the human state—which is expected to evolve still further. In the *Metaphysics*, Iqbal quotes that passage 'to show how successfully the poet anticipates the modern concept of evolution, which he regarded as the realistic side of his Idealism' (p. 91). In the *Reconstruction*, Iqbal's assessment of the value of the passage undergoes a change. Instead of calling Rumi a precursor of modern evolutionists, Iqbal now contrasts the philosophical implications of Rumi's thought with the despair-inducing thought of modern advocates of evolution: 'The theory of evolution, however, has brought despair and anxiety, instead of hope and enthusiasm for

life, to the modern world' (IV. 97). And just before he quotes
the passage, Iqbal remarks: 'The world of to-day needs a Rumi
to create an attitude of hope, and to kindle the fire of enthusiasm
for life' (97). In fact, Iqbal sees such a sharp divergence between
Rumi's view of evolution and the modern view of evolution that,
elsewhere in the *Reconstruction*, he expresses deep surprise that
the same idea should have affected Islamic and European culture
so differently (VII. 147–8).

3. *Metaphysics* as the Precursor of *Reconstruction*

In spite of the differences—and they are important—between the
two works, the *Metaphysics* can, in a sense, be called the precursor
of the *Reconstruction*. One who is familiar with the content, method,
and style of the scholarship of the *Metaphysics* will have little
difficulty in accepting that the *Reconstruction* is a later, and maturer,
product of the same pen. Work on the *Metaphysics* seems to have
equipped Iqbal with the tools of research necessary to undertake
more ambitious projects. It also anchored him in the Islamic and
Western traditions of learning. Finally, it reinforced his predilection
for engagement with serious issues and sharpened his critical
powers—thus launching him on a philosophical career whose
fruits included the *Reconstruction*.

5

Social and Political Thought

I. SOCIETY

1. Individual and Society

Iqbal discusses the relationship between society and the individual. Like an individual, society is an organism. In existential, functional, and teleological terms, it can be said to be prior to the individual: 'Society has a distinct life of its own, irrespective of the life of its component units taken individually'; it 'has or rather tends to have a consciousness, a will, and an intellect of its own'; 'the individual as such is a mere abstraction, a convenient expression for facility of social reference'; and everything about the individual is 'determined by the needs of the community of whose collective life he is only a partial expression', the individual's activity being 'nothing more than an unconscious performance of a particular function which social economy has allotted to him' (SWS, 119). Unlike the individual, society is 'infinite; it includes within its contents the innumerable unborn generations which . . . must be considered the most important portion of a living community', for 'in the successful group-life it is the future which must always control the present' (ibid. 120). The single most important problem for any society is 'the problem of a continuous national life', for every society seeks to perpetuate itself—to achieve immortality (ibid. 120–1).

But the primacy of society does not negate the importance of the individual: while society has a mind of its own, 'the stream of its mentality has no other channel through which to flow than individual minds' (SWS, 119). To Iqbal, in fact, 'every human being is a centre of latent power, the possibilities of which can be developed by cultivating a certain type of character' (SR, 139). Furthermore, not all people are equally powerful carriers or competent representatives of a society's traditions:

The legal, historical and literary traditions of a community . . . are definitely present to the consciousness of its lawyers, historians and literary writers, though the community as a whole is only vaguely conscious of them. (Ibid. 130)

Accordingly, Iqbal stresses the importance of rearing 'self-con-centrated individuals', for 'Such individuals alone reveal the depth of life' (Reconstruction, 120).

Does Iqbal, then, hold contradictory views on the relative importance of the individual and society? According to Iqbal, neither society nor the individual has absolute importance; society exists through and in the persons of individuals, but when individuals come together and form a society, they give rise to an entity that is larger than the aggregate of its members. Accordingly, Iqbal rejects a totalitarian system in which the individual's identity is suppressed, but he equally abhors unbridled individualism that undermines society's foundations. Ultimately, both society and the individual are supposed to submit to a higher ethical code—in Islamic terminology, this would be called submission to a revelation-based code. Instead of seeing society and the individual as rivals or competitors, this code seeks to streamline the efforts of individuals in order to create a unified social vision and, at the same time, to create a social environment that would allow its members to realize their personal potential in the most effective way. One can see that Iqbal holds society and individuals to be integrally related. While nations certainly outlast individuals—Iran, for example, survived the great king

Jamshed (*PM*, 240)—every individual can be the star of his nation's destiny (*AHf*, 657).

2. Decline of Muslim Societies: Causes

Given the importance of individuals who represent society and serve as its agents, society's progress or decline would, to a large extent, depend on the conduct of those individuals. In a short Urdu poem, Iqbal likens a nation to a body and the individuals comprising it to its limbs: those in industry are the nation's hands and feet, those who help to administer the government are its beautiful face, and those who cultivate arts—Iqbal mentions poets as representing this class—are its eyes (*BD*, 63). It follows that the failure of society's leaders or representatives can have disastrous consequences for the entire society. This understanding lies behind Iqbal's scathing critique of the leaders of historical Muslim societies. Iqbal holds the following three factors especially responsible for the general decadence of the Muslim world in recent centuries:

a. *Mullaism.* This is the name Iqbal gives to the hidebound attitude of the *mullas*, the conventional ulema, or religious scholars. Always 'a source of great strength to Islam', the ulema, 'during the course of centuries, especially since the destruction of Baghdad [1258], . . . became extremely conservative and would not allow any freedom of *ijtihad*, i.e. the forming of independent judgement in matters of law' (*SWS*, 231).

b. *Mysticism.* In the history of Muslim socieities, mysticism used to be, in the words of Iqbal, 'a force of spiritual education'. In later centuries it degenerated, cutting off Muslims from the actualities of life. Mystical practices increasingly became 'a mere means of exploiting the ignorance and the credulity of the people'. This was anomalous to 'the spirit of Islam . . . [which] aimed at the conquest of matter and not flight from it' (*SWS*, 231–2). At its origin in Arabia, Islam was a dynamic religion, but the influence of Persia robbed it of its virile character: 'The conquest of Persia meant not the conversion of Persia to Islam, but the conversion of Islam to Persianism' (ibid. 155). The Persian-influenced mysticism sought 'Reality in quarters where it does not exist': it delved into a distinction between the esoteric and the exoteric—between a true, inner Reality and a deceptive, outward Phenomenon—and thereby created in Muslims 'the tendency to ignore the Law—the only force holding together Moslem society', and replaced 'Moslem Democracy' with 'spiritual Aristocracy' (ibid. 154–5).

c. *Kingship*. Protection of their 'dynastic interests' being their first priority, Muslim kings 'did not hesitate to sell their countries to the highest bidder' (SWS, 232).

Regeneration of Muslim societies requires that the forces responsible for their decadence be combated. Modern Muslim reformers, like Jamal al-Din al-Afghani, Muhammad 'Abduh, and Zaghlul Pasha, 'found the world of Islam ruled by [the above-mentioned] three forces and they concentrated their whole energy on creating a revolt against these forces' (SWS, 231; also 232).

Iqbal's criticism of mullaism, mysticism, and kingship as the main factors responsible for the decadence of Muslim societies is not a blanket criticism of Muslim legists, mystics, and rulers. Iqbal held that, in early Islamic history, the three institutions of law, mysticism, and politics embodied, for varying lengths of time, the dynamic Islamic spirit. In later periods, however, the legists became prisoners of formalism, the mystics were seduced by a false dichotomy of spirit and matter, and the rulers sacrificed collective interest at the altar of personal gain. The fact that the same institutions can be, at one time, forces of progress and, at another time, forces of decadence, suggests that they need to and can be reformed. Therefore, instead of calling for a wholesale rejection of tradition, Iqbal aims at reinvigorating it—by subjecting it to critical scrutiny, with a view to retaining its kernel and discarding its husk.

Iqbal took a typically modern—which is to say, a historico-sociological—approach to the problems of Muslims in the world. In his article 'The Muslim Community—A Sociological Study', Iqbal, after pointing out the wretched economic condition of the average Indian Muslim, pointedly asks: 'Have we ever given a thought to these aspects of the social problems?' (SWS, 136). Instead of romanticising about the past glory of Islam or blaming foreign colonial powers for all the ills the Muslim world is heir to, Iqbal tries to examine the Muslim polity itself for the causes of Muslim backwardness and stagnation, his analysis leading him to identify institutional breakdown as the principal cause of Muslim political and social troubles. His unsparing critique of Muslim religious practice and political and social conduct proceeds from his conviction—stated in the Preface to *Rumuz-i Bikhudi* (1918) and elsewhere—that nations no less than individuals have an ego, or a self. And just as an individual's growth depends on the affirmation of the individual ego, so a nation's survival and development depend on the preservation of its national ego and of its national historical memory.

3. The Masses

The existence of competent leaders is crucial to a society's viability and progress, but so is the well-being—especially the economic well-being—of the masses. Referring to the Indian Muslim context, Iqbal stresses the need to improve 'the general condition of the masses of our community', noting that 'the economic condition of the average Muslim is extremely deplorable' (SWS, 135). 'It is the masses who are the backbone of the nation; they ought to be better fed, better housed and properly educated' (ibid. 109). Iqbal differs with those who hold the custom of *pardah* (veil worn by women, seclusion of women) responsible for the starving conditions of large sections of the community: 'It is really this poverty of the lower *strata* of our community and not the *Pardah* system, as our young protagonists of social reform sometimes contend, that is reacting on the general physique of our community' (ibid. 136). Muslim social organizations should realize that their main obligation is to elevate the masses, not to exalt individuals, and Muslim public workers need to study carefully the causes that have brought about 'the general economic situation of India' (ibid.).

The problem of economic backwardness must be 'approached

in a broad impartial, non-sectarian spirit, since the economic forces affect all communities alike' (SWR, 136). To this end, 'the public workers of all the communities [ought to] meet on the common ground of economic discussion' (ibid.). The Muslim public worker's preoccupation with securing more government jobs is misplaced, for government service 'offers prospects of economic elevation only to a few individuals; the general health of a community depends largely on its economic independence' (ibid. 136–7). In other words, 'there are other spheres of economic activity which are equally important and more profitable' (ibid. 137).

In Iqbal's view, a 'system of technical education [is] even more important than higher education' for such a system 'touches the general economic condition of the masses which form the backbone of a community, the latter only a few individuals who happen to possess more than average intellectual energy' (SWS, 137; also 245). The well-to-do must play their role in this respect: 'The charity of the wealthier classes among us must be so organized as to afford opportunities of a cheap technical education to the children of a community' (ibid. 137). At the same time, the close link between technical knowledge and ethical training must not be forgotten:

But industrial and commercial training alone is not sufficient. In economic competition the ethical factor plays an equally important part. The virtues of thrift, mutual trust, honesty, punctuality and co-operation are as much valuable economic assets as Professional skill. . . . If we want to turn out good working men, good shopkeepers, good artisans, and above all good citizens, we must first make them good Muslims. (Ibid.)

Iqbal's concern for the economic well-being of the general populace connects him with the eighteenth-century Indian Muslim scholar-reformer Shah Wali'ullah, who held that a just economic system is an integral part of a good society. Coming a century and a half after Shah Wali'ullah, and taking into account the phenomenon of the Russian Revolution of the early twentieth century as well as that of the Industrial Revolution that started in the late eighteenth century, Iqbal emphasizes the importance of technical education as a means of achieving general economic prosperity.

4. Culture, Character, and Education

Muslim communal life depends not only on the 'unity of religious belief', but also on 'the uniformity of Muslim Culture' (SWS, 125). Muslim culture is 'relatively universal' in the sense that it is not the product of a single race (ibid.). While the Arabs were largely responsible for Islam's early political expansion, it was, chiefly, the non-Arabs who gave Islam its 'enormous wealth of literature and thought' (ibid. 121–2). The contribution of Persia to Muslim culture is especially significant. 'The most important event in the history of Islam . . . [is] the conquest of Persia', for this conquest

gave to the Arabs not only a beautiful country, but also an ancient people who could construct a new civilisation out of the Semitic and the Aryan material. Our Muslim civilisation is a product of the cross-fertilisation of the Semitic and the Aryan ideas. It inherits the softness and refinement of its Aryan mother and the sterling character of its Semitic father. . . . But for Persia our culture would have been absolutely one-sided. (Ibid. 125–6)

Individual Muslims, in order to become living members of their community, 'must thoroughly assimilate the culture of Islam' (ibid. 126) if they are to 'feel the continuity of the present with the past and the future' (ibid. 129):

The object of this assimilation is to create a uniform mental outlook, a peculiar way of looking at the world, a definite standpoint from which to judge the value of things which sharply defines our community, and transforms it into a corporate individual, giving it a definite purpose and ideal of its own. (Ibid. 126)

Individuals who are grounded in Islamic culture will succeed in cultivating the Muslim type of character—the type that 'holds up the ideal of self-control, and is dominated by a more serious view of life' (ibid. 127). The Muslim personality type is to be distinguished from the valorous type, which is called forth by the struggle for existence that marks life in primitive societies. The Muslim character also differs from the convivial type, which partakes of 'the pleasures of life, and combines in itself the virtues of liberality, generosity and good fellowship' (ibid. 126–7).

At this point, one can clearly see the importance of education for building the typical Muslim character:

It must be the object of all our education to develop that type. If it is our aim to secure a continuous life of the community we must produce a type of character which, at all costs, holds fast to its own, and while it readily assimilates all that is good in other types, it carefully excludes from its life all that is hostile to its cherished traditions and institutions. (Ibid. 127)

Education, like other things, ought to be determined by the needs of the learner. A form of education which has no direct bearing on the particular type of character which you want to develop is absolutely worthless. (Ibid. 109)

Like the individual mind, the social mind has its personal identity, which is preserved by means of education. The social mind's continuity

is dependent on the orderly transmission of its continuity experience from generation to generation. The object of education is to secure this orderly transmission and thus to give a unity of self-consciousness of personal identity to the social mind. . . . The various portions of the collective tradition so transmitted by education permeate the entire social mind, and become objects of clear consciousness in the minds of a few individuals only whose life and thought become specialised for the various purposes of the community. (Ibid. 130)

On reviewing the Muslim system of education in India from this standpoint, Iqbal feels disappointed. He observes how the 'modern Muslim young man [is] a specimen of character whose intellectual life has absolutely no background of Muslim culture', for he has assimilated 'western habits of thoughts to an alarming extent', his mental life having become 'thoroughly demuslimised' (ibid.

130–1). 'In our educational enterprise we have hardly realized the truth . . . that an undivided devotion to an alien culture is a kind of imperceptible conversion to that culture' (ibid. 131). Our educational enterprise is driven by considerations of immediate economic gain, and so our educational products have little to commend themselves. Iqbal delivers the harsh verdict: 'The Muslim Student, ignorant of the social, ethical and political ideals that have dominated the mind of his community, is spiritually dead' (ibid.). We need to change our priorities: 'Economic considerations alone ought not to determine our activity as a people; the preservation of the unity of the community, the continuous national life is a far higher ideal than the service of merely immediate ends' (ibid. 132). Iqbal stresses the need for 'a teaching university of our own' (ibid. 133; also 110), urging, at the same time, that the 'scattered educational forces'—some conservatively religious, others relatively Westernized—'be organised into a central institution of a large purpose' (ibid. 133).

As for the education of Muslim women, Iqbal frankly remarks: 'It appears that Nature has allotted different functions to them, and a right performance of these functions is equally indispensable for the health and prosperity of the human family' (ibid. 134). Iqbal is unimpressed with the Western movement to emancipate women:

The so-called 'emancipation of the western woman' necessitated by western individualism and the peculiar economic situation produced by an unhealthy competition, is an experiment, in my opinion, likely to fail, not without doing incalculable harm, and creating extremely intricate social problems. (Ibid.)

He believes that

the Muslim woman should continue to occupy the position in society which Islam has allotted to her. And the position which has been allotted to her must determine the nature of her education. I have tried to show above that the solidarity of our community rests on our hold on the religion and culture of Islam. The woman is the principal depository of the religious idea. In the interests of a continuous national life, therefore, it is extremely necessary to give her, in the first place, a sound religious education. That, however, must be supplemented by a general knowledge of Muslim History, Domestic Economy, and Hygiene. This will enable her to give a degree of intellectual companionship to her husband, and successfully to do the duties of motherhood which, in my opinion, is the principal function of a woman. All subjects which have a tendency to de-womanise and to de-muslimise her must be carefully excluded from her education. (Ibid. 134–5)

Iqbal's views on education can be fully appreciated when they are put in the context of nineteenth-century India. In the wake of the establishment of British rule in India, Sir Sayyid Ahmad Khan was the first writer and reformer who tried to impress upon Muslims the need to acquire modern education for purposes of social advancement. Sir Sayyid's educational initiative led to the establishment, in north India, of a modern-style college whose Muslim graduates would be able to compete with non-Muslims for jobs in government and elsewhere. Iqbal admired Sayyid Ahmad Khan and his efforts to win back for Muslims their erstwhile status of honour in Indian society. But while he acknowledged the importance of education for a community's overall welfare and progress, he had philosophical differences with Sayyid Ahmad Khan on the objectives of education. To Iqbal, the fundamental purpose of education is not to turn out employable graduates, but to produce the type of character that would ensure society's survival and continuity. Judged by this yardstick, neither the traditional Islamic *madrasa* or seminary education nor the modern secular scheme of education would by itself seem to have much merit. Accordingly, the specifics of Iqbal's proposed educational programme for Muslims diverged sharply from those of Sir Sayyid's both in orientation and in scope. Sir Sayyid's reform programme was almost exclusively educational, whereas education formed only one plank—albeit an important one—of Iqbal's comprehensive scheme of social change. Unlike Sir Sayyid, Iqbal stressed the need for technical education for the masses and, more important, viewed education as an instrument not just of a certain type of individual character but also of a certain type of national mind-set—both informed by an Islamic ethical vision. Above all, Iqbal urged Muslims to make both a deep and critical study of their own cultural and intellectual tradition and a serious study of modern Western thought with a view to finding creative ways of reviving the Islamic legacy and making it relevant and viable in modern contexts. In other words, Iqbal believed that education could be used to bring about a veritable renaissance of thought in the Muslim world.

Iqbal's view of the role of Persia in Islamic history at first sight appears to be ambiguous, or even self-contradictory, but a closer look will present the matter in a different light. Iqbal speaks approvingly of the refining influence of Persia on the rugged Arabian character, yet he is critical of the enervating effect of Persian mysticism on Islamic culture. But this only means that Iqbal's evaluation of Persia's legacy is nuanced. He takes a similar view of the influence of the West on modern Islamic history. He is severely critical of certain aspects of Western culture and repeatedly warns Muslims to beware of imitating the West slavishly. At the same time, he admires certain other aspects of that culture, and, furthermore, regards as highly positive the role of the West in giving a wake-up call to the slumbering Muslim world.

II. POLITICS

The shock, despair, and cynicism from which the Muslims of India suffered after the Mughal Empire's demise in 1857 drove many of them into a state of passivity and inaction. Sayyid Ahmad Khan's attempt to reinvigorate the Muslim community by persuading it to take up the challenges posed by the new realities was initially resisted by the conservative religious establishment but, over the long run, achieved a fair degree of success. In the 1903 poem 'The Sayyid's Tombstone' (*BD*, 52–3), Iqbal says that Islam does not teach Muslims to renounce the world. The poem also has a line, 'Courage is the staff in the politicians' hands' (Urdu: *Hai daleri dast-i arbab-i siyasat ka 'asa)*', which prefigures Iqbal's frequent use of the image of Moses' staff as a symbol of power—often political power. At this time, however, politics was not a major concern for him, and the few poems of this early period that are expressly nationalistic or patriotic (for example, 'Indian Anthem' (BD, 83); 'Indian Children's National Song' (BD, 87); and 'New Temple' (BD, 88)) do not reflect any systematically worked out political views.

At the turn of the century, Iqbal, like most Indian Muslims—or rather, like most other Indians—must have observed with interest the political developments that were taking place in the country. Furthermore, several of the Muslim social organizations with which Iqbal was closely associated aimed not only at protecting Muslims' rights as a religious community, but also at promoting Muslim education and creating a general—not excluding political—awareness among Muslims. It seems, however, that Iqbal became seriously interested in political matters only during his stay in Europe, where he got the opportunity not only to study European political thought, but also to examine and assess the disastrous consequences for European powers of pursuit of nationalist policies on the continent, and of their (often ruthless) imperialist policies abroad. In England, Iqbal gave a series of talks on diverse Islamic topics, including Islamic political topics, but, unfortunately, no record of the talks exists. In 1908, a British Committee of the All-India Muslim League (founded in Dacca in 1906) was set up, and Iqbal was appointed its secretary. Soon after his return from England, political themes began to assume greater significance in both his prose and his poetry. For example, in the third part of Bang-i Dara, which contains poems written from 1908 onwards, the poems 'Islamic Anthem' (BD, 159) and 'Nationalism' (BD, 160–1; this poem is subtitled 'Nation as a Political Concept') signify a rejection of the modern notion of territorial nationalism and an espousal of Islam as furnishing a basis of nationality. This view is set forth in many of Iqbal's later poems and also in a number of his prose works.

At times, Iqbal took part in practical politics in a limited way. In his post-Europe career, he gave talks and addresses at numerous rallies held to voice Muslim public opinion not only on domestic political matters, but also on international issues affecting the wider Islamic world. In 1926, he was elected a member of the Punjab Legislative Council; for several years, he served as president of the Punjab Muslim League; in 1931 and 1932, he represented India's Muslims at two of the three Round Table Conferences held in London to discuss India's future constitutional status; and, for almost three decades, he was in dialogue with many of India's distinguished political leaders. But perhaps his most enduring contribution to politics consists in his writings on the subject—essays, letters, addresses, and statements—that contain not only analysis and commentary, but also a series of constructive proposals. Notable among his political writings are three essays, 'Political Thought in Islam' (1908), 'Islam as a Moral and Political Ideal' (1909), and 'The Muslim Community—A Sociological Study' (1910); two presidential addresses, one given at the annual session of the All-India Muslim League (1930) and the other at the annual session of the All-India Muslim Conference (1932); and the fifth and sixth lectures in *The Reconstruction of Religious Thought in Islam*. The three essays and the two presidential addresses are included in Latif Sherwani's compilation, *Speeches, Writings and Statements of Iqbal*, from which we have already cited above.

1. Nationalism and Islam

Iqbal was severely critical of the modern Western concept of nation-state. In the poem 'Nationalism', Iqbal remarks that modern nationalism divides up humankind into artificial entities that, motivated by greed and selfishness, wage unprincipled and bloody wars with one another for control of economic resources. A number of poems in *Zarb-i Kalim* contain bitter diatribes on the havoc wrought in the world by the self-considering, jingoistic nationalism of the so-called civilized countries. In the West, the separation of religion and state, by lifting all moral restraint from the state, has turned the latter into a Frankentein's monster: 'The divorce of religion from politics results in Genghizship', runs one of Iqbal's best-known lines of poetry (*BJ*, 332). For Muslims, religion is central to life. 'The religious idea . . . determines the ultimate structure of the Muslim Community' (*SWS*, 123). Iqbal writes:

Islam has a far deeper significance for us than merely religious, it has a peculiarly national meaning, so that our communal life is unthinkable without a firm grasp of the Islamic Principle. The idea of Islam is, so to speak, our eternal home or country wherein we live, move and have our being. To us it is above everything else, as England is above all to the Englishman and *Deutschland über alles* to the German. The moment our grasp of the Islamic Principle is loosened that solidarity of our community is gone. (Ibid. 124–5)

This being so, one can expect Islam to furnish a distinctive basis for nationality. This, in fact, is the case, according to Iqbal:

The essential difference between the Muslim Community and other Communities of the world consists in our peculiar conception of nationality. It is not the unity of language or country or the identity of economic interest that constitutes the basic principle of our nationality. It is because we all believe in a certain view of the universe, and participate in the same historical tradition that we are members of the society founded by the Prophet of Islam. Islam abhors all material limitations, and bases its nationality on a purely abstract idea, objectified in a potentially expansive group of concrete personalities. It is not dependent for its life-principle on the character and genius of a particular people; in its essence it is non-temporal, non-spatial. (Ibid. 121)

Iqbal's view of the centrality of religion in life, including political life, is predicated on the philosophical conviction that the Ultimate Reality is spiritual in character and 'its life consists in its temporal activity' (*Reconstruction*, VI, 123), and that 'matter is spirit in space-time reference' (ibid. 122). Iqbal says:

The essence of *Tauhid* [Islamic monotheism], as a working idea, is equality, solidarity, and freedom. The state, from the Islamic standpoint, is an endeavour to transform these ideal principles into space-time forces, an aspiration to realize them in a definite human organization. It is in this sense alone that the state in Islam is a theocracy, not in the sense that it is headed by a representative of God on earth who can always screen his despotic will behind his supposed infallibility. . . . The state, according to Islam, is only an effort to realize the spiritual in a human organization. But in this sense all state, not based on mere domination and aiming at the realization of ideal principles, is theocratic. (Ibid. 122–3)

The universal ideals of freedom, equality, and solidarity suggest that the ultimate objective of Islam is the establishment of a 'spiritual democracy' (ibid. 142), one that is uncircumscribed by any consideration of territoriality.

Iqbal's rejection of territoriality as the basis of nationality and his notion of spiritual democracy might suggest that, in his view, Islam is hostile to the idea of individual sovereign nations. This is not necessarily the case. While 'The political ideal of Islam consists in the creation of a people born of a free fusion of all races and nationalities' (SWS, 141), the 'ideal nation . . . is not incompatible with the sovereignty of individual States, since its structure will be determined not by physical force, but by the spiritual force of a common ideal' (ibid. 143). Islam's repudiation of territorial nationalism—or, conversely, its espousal of universal Muslim solidarity—does not necessarily imply that a transnational state is the only form the Islamic political vision can take. The crucial fact about the Islamic vision is that it is spiritual in character. Islamic solidarity

facilitates the political combination of Muslim States, which combination may either assume the form of a world-State (ideal) or of a league of Muslim States, or of a number of independent States whose pacts and alliances are determined by purely economic and political considerations. (Ibid. 238)

Under the present circumstances, in any case, 'every Muslim nation must sink into her own deeper self, temporarily focus her vision on herself alone, until all are strong and powerful to form a living family of republic' (Reconstruction, VI, 126). Philosophically, 'the Muslim Commonwealth is based on the principle of absolute equality of all Muslims in the eyes of the law' (SWS, 140; also

116). It is also based on the principle of the unity of religious and secular authority. The caliph, however, is 'not necessarily the high-priest of Islam', being subject, like any other individual, 'to the impersonal authority of the law' (ibid. 141–2).

As for the historical formulations of Islamic political theory, Iqbal regards them as Muslim legists' transmutation of such pre-Islamic political customs as pertained to tribal succession (SWS, 138–9). Iqbal discusses the 'three great political theories' (ibid. 142) which emerged early in Islam—namely, the Sunni theory of elective monarchy, the Shi'i theory of government, by divine right, of the infallible imam, and the Khariji theory of republican government (ibid. 143–54). In his view, 'the fundamental principle laid down in the Qur'an is the principle of election'. But there were two reasons why the idea 'did not develop on strictly Islamic lines': it was 'not at all suited to the genius of the Persians and the Mongols—the two principal races which accepted Islam as their religion', and the continuous political expansion in the early period tended 'to concentrate political power in fewer hands' (ibid. 153). Iqbal regards democracy as 'the most important aspect of Islam regarded as a political ideal' (ibid. 115). Under the impact of Western political thought, 'Muslim countries have exhibited signs of political life', but Muslim political reformers need 'to make a thorough study of Islamic constitutional principles' (ibid. 153), for then they will be able to show that 'their seemingly borrowed ideal of political freedom is really the ideal of Islam' (ibid. 154).

A review of Iqbal's ideas on nationalism shows that Iqbal is searching for a viable basis of Muslim political unity in the context of modern times. He tries to remain faithful to the conception of Islam as a code of law that furnishes guidance in all spheres of life, including the political. Nevertheless, he is cognizant of the need to react in a meaningful way to the paradigmatic changes that have occurred, under Western civilizational domination, in both political theory and political practice. He identifies certain meeting points between Islamic and Western political concepts. For example, his statement that the Qur'an lays great stress on the principle of election is intended to show that Islamic political doctrine is, in some respect, consonant with the reigning Western political doctrine, and to suggest that, in adopting the Western concept of election, Muslims will be embracing part of their own tradition. Iqbal is, however, careful to base his argument in this regard on the primary textual source of Islam, the Qur'an; he not only rejects the centuries-old Muslim historical practice of dynasticism, he subjects it to severe critique. In fact, when he says that the historical formulations of Islamic political theory should be viewed as Muslim legal scholars' 'transmutations' of pre-Islamic Arabian political customs, he throws the door wide open for a fresh formulation of Muslim political theory in the light of today's circumstances.

Iqbal is often called a pan-Islamist, but this can be misleading. Iqbal wished to unify the Muslims of the world, but their unification, in his view, would have a spiritual rather than a geographical basis. He nowhere proposes that the existing Muslim countries should abolish their borders and create a universal Muslim state ruled by a single caliph. He grants the possibility of the simultaneous existence of many Muslim states and of many Muslim rulers. His proposal about the creation of a Muslim League of Nations, too, presupposes the existence of multiple Muslim states that have freely chosen to become members of an organization in order jointly to pursue common objectives. In a 1933 statement, Iqbal explained his view of pan-Islamism. He distinguishes between pan-Islamism as a political idea and as a humanitarian ideal. The first he rejects, asserting that even Jamal al-Din al-Afghani (the putative originator of the idea of pan-Islamism) 'never dreamed of a unification of Muslims into a political State' (SWS, 282). The second he accepts unreservedly, though he would, in this case, replace the term 'pan-Islamism' with 'Islam':

It is, however, true that Islam as a society or as a practical scheme for the combination not only of race but also of all religions does not recognise the barriers of race and nationality or geographical frontiers. In the sense of this humanitarian ideal Pan-Islamism—if one prefers to use this unnecessarily long phrase to the simple expression 'Islam'—does and will always exist. (Ibid. 283–4)

2. The Indian Political Scene

Much of Iqbal's political thought deals with the situation of Muslims in India. It is well known that, for a period of time, he was a proponent of Indian nationalism: several of his early poems celebrate the ancient land of the Himalayas, the famous figures of Indian history, and the multicultural fabric of India, and he had hoped that the nations composing the Indian populations—especially the Hindus and the Muslims—would be able to live side by side in harmony and peace. But political developments in the country led him to remark that 'India's most difficult problem [is] the communal problem' (ibid. 14), namely, the problem of the conflict-ridden relationship between Hindus and Muslims. Eventually, he was convinced that 'the essential disparity between the two cultural units of India' (ibid. 25) would not permit the hoped-for coexistence. In his presidential address at the annual session of the All-India Muslim League held at Allahabad in 1930, Iqbal proposed the creation of a state for the Muslims of India:

I would like to see the Punjab, North-West Frontier Province, Sind and Baluchistan amalgamated into a single state. Self-government within the British Empire, or without the British Empire, the formation of a consolidated North-West Indian Muslim state appears to me to be the final destiny of the Muslims, at least of North-West India. (Ibid. 11)

This passage is the first clearly formulated basis of what later became a demand for a separate homeland for the Muslims of India—a demand that led to the creation of Pakistan in 1947.

Besides providing the ideological impetus for the creation of a homeland for India's Muslims, Iqbal took practical steps to unite Indian Muslims under one political banner. In the first place, he strove to make the Muslim League the representative political party of the country's Muslims. He had to fight some political battles with rival Muslim groups to attain his goal. In the second place, he was instrumental, along with a few other people, in persuading Muhammad Ali Jinnah to again become active in practical politics and provide much-needed leadership to India's Muslims; Jinnah later became the founder of Pakistan. Iqbal's letters to Jinnah, written between May 1936 and November 1937, throw light on Iqbal's role in organizing the Muslim League in the Punjab. In his Foreword to the *Letters of Iqbal to Jinnah*, Jinnah acknowledged Iqbal's contribution in making the League the foremost political party of India's Muslims and established a direct link between Iqbal's views and the Lahore Resolution of 1940 (pp. 6–7), which officially launched the Pakistan movement. Building on his 1930 proposal about the creation of a Muslim state in India's northwest, Iqbal in these letters speaks of the Muslims of Bengal, too, as a nation 'entitled to self-determination' (p. 24). The *Letters* also indicates the important position that Indian Muslims, in Iqbal's view, held within the world Muslim polity. To Iqbal, 'the whole future of Islam as a moral and political force in Asia rests very largely on a complete organisation of Indian Muslims' (p. 13). As in some of his other writings, Iqbal in the *Letters* describes preservation of Muslim cultural identity as the first priority of India's Muslims (p. 14). In taking this position, he seeks to rebut Pandit Jawaharlal Nehru's contention that India's principal problem is economic, and that India's Muslims should, instead of organizing themselves as a separate political entity, work in concert with Hindus to solve the problem of poverty in India. In fact, Iqbal argues that the problem of Muslim poverty can be solved only through the enforcement of Islamic law, which guarantees each individual's right to subsistence; the enforcement of Islamic law, in turn, requires the establishment of one or more free Muslim states (pp. 17–8). Calling Jinnah 'the only Muslim in India today to whom the community has a right to look up for safe guidance through the storm which is coming to North-West India, and perhaps to the whole of India' (pp. 20–1), Iqbal advises that the Muslim League, in order to be strong and successful, ought to rely on Muslim masses rather than on elite Muslim groups (pp. 16–17, 18).

Iqbal's letters to Jinnah form an important document in the history of Muslim India. They indicate that Iqbal's conviction about Indian Muslims' entitlement to self-government, a conviction he first expressed in 1930, became stronger with the years, and that Iqbal played a pivotal role in changing the character of the Muslim League—from an elitist to a popular party. They also show that Iqbal sought to solve political problems by putting them in the larger, societal context; he saw a clear connection between politics, economics, and culture. The letters also give us a glimpse of Iqbal's personality. 'From them', says Sheila McDonough, 'we can see the unfailing courtesy and kindliness of Iqbal's manner of giving guidance, as well as his purposiveness' (*The Authority of the Past*, p. 18).

We noted above Iqbal's identification of pan-Islamism with humanitarianism. Is Iqbal's humanitarianism—or what some call his universalism—in conflict with Iqbal's localism, namely, with Iqbal's demand for a homeland for Indian Muslims? Iqbal's reply to a similar issue raised by some critics about his poetry drew a response from Iqbal himself:

The humanitarian ideal is always universal in poetry and philosophy; but if you make it an effective ideal and work it out in actual life, you must start, not with poets and philosophers, but with a society exclusive, in the sense of having a creed and a well-defined outline, but ever enlarging its limits by example and persuasion. (Iqbal's letter to Nicholson, in Hassan, *The Sword and the Sceptre*, p. 364.)

In other words, a universal vision, if it has to have an impact on life as lived on earth, must be captured in a local context. India's peculiar political circumstances seem to have convinced Iqbal that, in India at least, the universal ideals of Islam could be best actualized within the framework of a Muslim state.

Iqbal's social and political ideas flow directly from his con-viction that Islam is not only a creed but also a polity; that it not only presents a 'religious ideal' but also creates a 'social order' in accordance with that ideal (*SWS*, 8). The organic relationship between the abstract ideal and its institutional embodiment necessitates that an effort be made to translate that ideal into social reality, but also that the social reality be monitored in order to evaluate its conformity with the ideal. It is in the light of this understanding that Iqbal both underscores the importance of Islamic ideals as a source of inspiration and criticizes the prevailing conditions in the Muslim countries as falling short of the ideal. But there is no single paradigm of the interplay between the ideal and the real. The Islamic religious idea of nationality, for example, may work itself out in different ways in countries with different demographic realities or economic conditions. Similarly, the Muslims in a Muslim-minority country may have to accept a different political arrangement than the Muslims in a Muslim-majority country. And the common menace of poverty would necessitate intercommunal cooperation between Muslims and non-Muslims living in the same land. In other words, a religious outlook must take into account and accommodate practical realities of life.

Iqbal typically takes what may be called an integralist approach to issues (see Chapter 4, Section II.B). In studying society and prescribing a course of action for it, he assigns importance both to socio-economic factors and to religious ideals and ethical norms. He strongly believes, for example, that moral virtues play an important role in economic competition—and the search for moral virtues brings him to Islam as a system of thought and conduct. In his view, a society's problems are not exclusively political, economic, *or* ethical in character, but simultaneously have political, economic, *and* ethical dimensions, and their solution requires that they be seen in their complexity.

6

Iqbal's Legacy

It is generally granted that Iqbal is both one of the most significant and one of the most influential Muslim writers and thinkers of modern times. His poetry, especially, captivated the hearts and minds not only of general audiences who heard it recited in large gatherings or read it as text, but also of scholars, intellectuals, and other distinguished figures from various walks of life. Iqbal's works not only excited admiration, they also served as a catalyst to action. India's famous Ali Brothers—Muhammad Ali Jawhar (d. 1931) and Shawkat Ali (d. 1938)—found solace and inspiration in Iqbal's poetry during their imprisonment for anti-British activities. Muhammad Ali Jawhar famously said that he and other Muslim leaders of India learnt the true meaning of Islam from Iqbal's works, and Muhammad Ali Jinnah acknowledged Iqbal's seminal role in shaping Muslim identity in India and in directing the movement of thought and action that culminated in the creation of Pakistan. Several Pakistani organizations, some of them government-sponsored, seek to promote Iqbal studies. In Pakistan, selections from Iqbal's works, especially his poetry, are included in school and college curricula; a fairly large number of research papers and doctoral theses on Iqbal have been, and are being, written at universities; a stream of books dealing with Iqbal's life and his thought rolls off the press every year; annual Iqbal Day celebrations are held with great fervour and reverence; and, not to be left behind, singers sing Iqbal's poems to the accompaniment of music and painters try to capture Iqbal's ideas on canvas. In the larger world, too, Iqbal's distinction as a poet and as a philosopher has been recognized. Iqbal's works have been translated not only into many Islamic, but also into many Western languages; intellectual and literary figures of international stature have paid tribute to him; and Iqbal specialists teach and write in several Western countries.

But in spite of all the attention and admiration Iqbal has commanded, whether in the Indian subcontinent or in the world at large, one has the nagging feeling that his works have not yet received the kind of critical attention and appreciation they deserve. For one thing, many of the works published about him fail to come to grips with his multifaceted thought as expressed in his poetry and, especially, in his philosophical writings. The small number of really worthwhile works written in Urdu cry out—in vain—for a translation. For another, Iqbal is often evaluated in comparison with other well-known—mostly European—thinkers, such as Nietzsche, Bergson, Goethe, and Dante. Such comparative assessments imply that an independent canon of Iqbal study has yet to come into existence. Nevertheless, current Iqbal studies do seem to be developing a focus somewhat different from the earlier ones. More than once Iqbal 'disclaimed' the title of poet. He said that his primary concern was to present a certain set of ideas rather than to versify; he even said that he did not wish to be remembered as a poet. Iqbal, to be sure, was not unaware of his poetic gift, but the emphasis he put on his thought rather than on his poetic craft tells us something important about his own perception of his calling. When he denied that he was a poet, he meant that he should not be regarded as a poet in the conventional sense of the word, since he did not subscribe to the notion of poetry for poetry's sake but used poetry only as a vehicle of thought. Until now, Iqbal has been mainly viewed as a poet and the serious philosophical aspect of his thought, whether expressed in his prose or in his poetry, has not been fully recognized. That aspect has now begun to attract greater attention, and this changing trend is due, at least in part, to Western scholars' analytical and critical studies on Iqbal. As this trend solidifies, greater attention will be paid to Iqbal's prose works, many of them in English, and, one hopes, a new synthesis of Iqbal studies, based on a more balanced study of his poetical and prose works, will emerge.

Iqbal can easily be classed as a modern Muslim reformer. The distinction of his reformist thought is threefold: (1) it takes an integralist view of Islam, affirming it both as doctrine and as practice—or as religion and as culture—and establishing a strong link between these two aspects; (2) it is dynamic in not only admitting the possibility, but also underlining the necessity, of reinterpreting the content of Islamic tradition; (3) it is open-ended, in that it admits of interaction between Islamic and non-Islamic traditions. These points call for some elaboration.

Both in his explanation of historical developments in Islam and in his proposals for the uplift of Muslims, Iqbal is cognizant of the organic relationship between the various spheres of human life and activity. Thus, unlike those modern Muslim thinkers who consider education to be the panacea for all the ills of the Muslim world; unlike those who regard liberation of Muslim lands from Western colonial rule as the main desideratum of progress for Muslim nations; and unlike those who believe that economic development alone will solve the problems of the Muslim world—unlike all these thinkers, Iqbal stands for a comprehensive reform that will bring about change in all spheres of Muslim life—religious, intellectual, social, political, and economic. He maintains that a fundamental change in the spiritual outlook and cultural attitudes is a prerequisite for societal and institutional change, and that Muslims must address issues of general poverty and backwardness if they hope to bring about real change in society. In the same vein, he repeatedly lays stress on the social and cultural significance of such Islamic doctrines as monotheism.

Iqbal has articulated, perhaps more eloquently than any other Muslim writer in modern times, the notion that 'deed' rather than 'idea' has primary importance in the Qur'anic scheme of things.

The insight, which lies at the heart of Iqbal's thought, may be called one of Iqbal's enduring contributions to the study of Islam. It has both a critical and a constructive aspect. On its critical side, it enables Iqbal to reject the speculative Greek philosophy; on its constructive side, it leads him to emphasize the central role that Islamic law has played in the past and can play in the future in unifying the Muslim community. With its implications fully worked out, the insight will be seen to represent a convergence point for much of Iqbal's thought as expressed in his prose and poetry.

Iqbal would seem to represent, more crisply than any other modern Muslim thinker, the attitude that today's Muslims might adopt, caught as they are in the conflict between tradition and modernity. Iqbal seems to embrace both tradition and modernity— each with a sympathetic but critical eye. He declares, passionately and unabashedly, his loyalty to the religion of Islam and offers illuminating observations on the significance of such doctrinal propositions as the finality of Muhammad's prophethood. At the same time, he distinguishes between the eternal or essential and the historical or incidental in the Islamic tradition, and, invoking *ijtihad*, which he terms the principle of movement in Islam, calls upon Muslims to undertake a reconstruction of the Islamic tradition in the light of modern developments in all fields of knowledge and thought. His strong faith in the possibility of ultimate reconciliation of religion and science; his demonstration, in many cases, of the compatibility between Islamic religious propositions and modern scientific postulates; and, finally, his attempt to integrate Islamic and Western elements in his intellectual as well as in his practical life make him out to be a figure whom Muslims—both those of a traditional and those of a modern background—can respect and emulate.

The debate as to whether Iqbal was an Islamic thinker in a narrow sense or whether he was a cosmopolitan thinker almost amounts to hijacking the essence of Iqbal's thought. Just as it is a mistake to think that only that language with no roots in a particular culture or no association with a particular people can be truly international (the case of Esperanto comes to mind), so it is a mistake to think that only a writer or thinker who is not associated with a particular tradition or nation can be truly cosmopolitan. Local reference is not exclusive of universality. Iqbal's greatness consists in interpreting the spirit of Islamic culture in a way that shows Islam to be a dynamic, forward-looking, and all-encompassing movement that not only has profound meaning for those who believe in the religion, but also promises to serve as a force for good in the world at large. In the overall philosophical perspective of Iqbal, the caravan of human thought and experience is a single caravan, of which all peoples and races are members. This conviction makes Iqbal note with pride that modern Western culture represents the development of some of the aspects of Islamic culture. It also makes him say, without hurting his pride in the least, that Muslims today could equally benefit from the modern West's wealth of knowledge and experience.

In the history of modern thought—when that history deigns to recognise the merit of the works of non-Western thinkers—Iqbal will be remembered as one who mounted a spirited defence of the possibility of religion in a so-called scientific age. The boldness of Iqbal's approach is striking. Instead of offering an apology for religion and claiming that it is too abstruse or recondite a matter to be examined by philosophy, he challenges philosophy to study religion as an attempt to approach Reality as a whole. At the same time, Iqbal, far from rehashing the old arguments for the existence of God or of a spiritual realm, redefines the terms of the argument. He places his primary reliance on experience. While granting the normalcy of sense-perception, and of scientific knowledge based on sense-perception, he maintains that other, equally natural modes of knowledge exist. He rejects the notion that religious or mystic experience is by definition arcane or mysterious, holding, instead, that such experience is as open to critical scrutiny as the so-called scientific knowledge. Iqbal's attempt to bridge the perceived methodological gap between religion and philosophy is an important contribution to epistemology.

But perhaps Iqbal's most enduring legacy consists in his zestful affirmation of life. A study of Iqbal's life reveals that he was interested in practically everything that life had to offer. He read much, he thought much, he dreamed much, and he hoped much; he corresponded with many people, he had made close friendships with many people from many different communities and nationalities, and, above all, he was open to new ideas. His readers find his works inspiring. No less inspiring to them is his decidedly positive attitude to life.

Further Reading

Though only works written in English will be listed, I would like to mention, as a token of my appreciation, at least three of the Urdu works that have aided me in preparing this volume: Yusuf Husayn Khan's *Ruh-i Iqbal* (Lahore: Al-Qamar Enterprises, 6th edn. 1966; first published 1942); Aziz Ahmad's *Na'i Tashkil* (Lahore: Globe Publishers, 2nd edn. 1968); and Khalifah Abdul-Hakim's *Fikr-i Iqbal* (Lahore: Bazm-i Iqbal, 1988; first published 1957). A good project for an Iqbal scholar would be to translate into English selections from these and other Urdu works on Iqbal.

In a 1966 article, Robert Whittemore, in referring to Iqbal, remarked that one would 'seek in vain through the pages of most modern European and American philosophy for a mention of his name. He is unknown even to the compilers of philosophical dictionaries and encyclopedias' (in Waheed Quraishi (ed.), *Selections from The Iqbal Review* (Lahore: Iqbal Academy Pakistan, 1983), p. 257). The situation has changed since. In the last few decades, Iqbal has been studied by a number of scholars in the West. And, to be sure, he is now being mentioned and discussed in philosophical encyclopedias, dictionaries, and handbooks published in Western countries. For example, in Robert L. Arrington's edited volume *A Companion to the Philosophers* (Oxford: Blackwell, 1999), Iqbal is one of the eight philosophers included in the section on Islamic and Jewish philosophers, and he is in respectable company in Diané Collinson, Kathry Plant, and Robert Wilkinson's *Fifty Eastern Thinkers* (London: Routledge, 2000). Iqbal's principal philosophical work is *The Reconstruction of Religious Thought in Islam*, and study of this seminal work of modern Muslim thought has been facilitated by Saeed Sheikh's detailed annotation to the volume (see Iqbal's Texts Cited).

The bibliographies in Annemarie Schimmel's *Gabriel's Wing: A Study into the Religious Ideas of Sir Muhammad Iqbal* (Lahore: Iqbal Academy Pakistan, 2nd edn. 1989; first published 1963), and in Hafeez Malik (ed.), *Iqbal, Poet-Philosopher of Pakistan* (New York: Columbia University Press, 1971) are still valuable. There is, however, a great need for an updated and annotated bibliography, especially one that reviews works published in English and other Western languages.

A detailed biography of Iqbal in English is urgently needed. Based as it is on primary sources, Javed Iqbal's Urdu biography of his father, *Zindah-Rud* (*The Living Stream*; Lahore: Sheikh Ghulam Ali & Sons, 1989), is indispensable for any future research not only on Iqbal's life, but also on the background to his thought; an English translation, even an abridged one, would be a great boon. Atiya Begum, one of Iqbal's friends during his stay in Europe, reproduces in her *Iqbal* (Lahore: A'ina-i-Adab, 1977; first published 1947) a number of Iqbal's letters to her and also gives her 'impressions of his scholastic career in Europe'.

The number of well-written book-length introductions to Iqbal in English is small. Syed Abdul Vahid's highly readable *Iqbal, His Art and Thought* (London: John Murray, 1959) deals mostly with Iqbal's poetry, from which the author cites and translates extensive passages. The same author's *Glimpses of Iqbal* (Karachi: Iqbal Academy Pakistan, 1974) consists of interesting short essays on a variety of subjects, including an essay on Iqbal as a teacher and another on translating Iqbal. Iqbal Singh's *The Ardent Pilgrim* (New Delhi: Oxford University Press, 2nd edn. 1997; first published 1951) is helpful in explaining the larger background of ideas and political developments, both in India and in Europe, that shaped the age of Iqbal. The second edition is, however, marred by its insinuating attacks on Iqbal's personal life, and makes one wonder whether it is an improvement on the first edition (see Sheila McDonough's detailed review in *Studies in Contemporary Islam*, 3 (2001), 2:83–9). Riffat Hassan's *An Iqbal Primer: An Introduction to Iqbal's Philosophy* (Lahore: Aziz Publishers, 1979), written as a 'preliminary preparation' for her doctoral study, 'The Main Philosophical Ideas in the Writings of Muhammad Iqbal (1877–1938)', provides short but solid introductions to the individual prose and poetical works of Iqbal; the introductions are followed by a chapter on Iqbal's philosophical ideas. Luce-Claude Maitre's *Introduction to the Thought of Iqbal*, trans. Mulla Abdul Majid Dar (Karachi: Iqbal Academy, 1961) offers a brief but useful overview. Lini S. May's *Iqbal: His Life and Times 1877–1938* (Lahore: Sh. Muhammad Ashraf, 1974) provides a fact-filled and quotation-rich account of the times in which Iqbal lived and wrote. Alam Khundmiri's lucidly written essays on Iqbal make up Part iii of M. T. Ansari (ed.), *Secularism, Islam and Modernity: Selected Essays of Alam Khundmiri* (New Delhi: Sage Publications, 2001). But the best general introduction to Iqbal remains Schimmel's *Gabriel's Wing*.

Several edited volumes provide informative and critical perspectives on Iqbal: *Iqbal as a Thinker: Essays by Eminent Scholars* (Lahore: Sh. Muhammad Ashraf, 1944); Hafeez Malik (ed.), *Iqbal, Poet-Philosopher of Pakistan* (New York: Columbia University Press, 1971); M. Saeed Sheikh (ed.), *Studies in Iqbal's Thought and Art: Select Articles from the Quarterly 'Iqbal'* (Lahore: Bazm-i Iqbal, 1972); Asloob Ahmad Ansari, *Iqbal: Essays and Studies* (New Delhi: Ghalib Academy, 1978); Waheed Quraishi (ed.), *Selections from the Iqbal Review* (Lahore: Iqbal Academy, 1983); and Ali Sardar Jafri and K. S. Duggal, eds., *Iqbal: Commemorative Volume* (New Delhi: All India Iqbal Centenary Celebrations Committee [after 1977]). Mention must also be made of Riffat Hassan's *The Sword and the Sceptre* (Lahore: Iqbal Academy Pakistan, 1977), which includes a number of classic essays on Iqbal's poetry that are no longer easily available.

To come to article-length treatments of Iqbal: Annemarie Schimmel provides a summary account of Iqbal's life and works in *Islam in the Subcontinent* (Leiden: E. J. Brill, 1980), pp. 223–35. Aziz Ahmad offers a synoptic view of Iqbal's philosophical, religious, and political thought in *Islamic Modernism in India and Pakistan 1857–1964* (London: Oxford University Press, 1967), pp. 141–63. Sheila McDonough, in *The Authority of the Past: A Study of Three Muslim Modernists* (Chambersburg, Pennsylvania: American Academy of Religion, 1971), pp. 16–34, gives an account of Iqbal's basic philosophical ideas and also compares some of his ideas with Sayyid Ahmad Khan's. Muhammad Sadiq discusses Iqbal's Urdu poetry at some length, with copious illustrations, in *A History of Urdu Literature* (London: Oxford University Press, 1964), pp. 357–89. On a smaller scale, Schimmel treats Iqbal's Persian poetry in Ehsan Yarshater (ed.), *Persian Literature* (Albany, New York: State University of New York Press, 1988), pp. 422–7. Robert D. Lee examines Iqbal's thought from certain thematic perspectives in *Overcoming Tradition and Modernity: The Search for Islamic Authenticity* (Boulder, Colorado: Westview Press, 1977), pp. 57–82. Two encyclopaedia articles on Iqbal are Annemarie Schimmel, 'Ikbal', in the second edition of the *Encyclopaedia of Islam* (Leiden: E. J. Brill, 1960, continuing), iii. 1057–9, and Hafeez Malik, 'Iqbal, Muhammad', in John L. Esposito (ed.), *The Oxford Encyclopedia of the Modern Muslim World*, 5 vols. (New York and Oxford: Oxford University Press, 1995), ii. 221–4. Volume 28 of *Twentieth-Century Literary Criticism* (Detroit: Gale Research Company, 1988) devotes a section to Iqbal (178–206); it contains excerpts from the works of several writers and critics, including E. M. Forster, Alessandro Bausani, Syed Abdul Vahid, Faiz A. Faiz, and John L. Esposito.

Several of Iqbal's individual poetry volumes have been rendered into English (see the bibliographies in Malik and Schimmel), but the translations frequently raise questions of accuracy and quality. Anthologies of Iqbal's poetry include V. G. Kiernan, *Poems from Iqbal* (London: John Murray, 2nd edn. 1955); D. J. Matthews, *Iqbal: A Selection of the Urdu Verse—Text and Translation* (London:

University of London School of Oriental and African Studies, 1993); and Mustansir Mir, *Tulip in the Desert: A Selection of the Poetry of Muhammad Iqbal* (London: Hurst; Montreal: Queens-McGill University Press; and New Delhi: Orient Longman, 2000). Matthews' work, as the title indicates, includes Iqbal's Urdu poems. Kiernan adds a few poems from the Persian *Payam-i Mashriq* as well. In both, the poems from any single work of Iqbal's are presented as a block, with the blocks arranged in the books' chronological order. Mir's anthology is thematically arranged and contains translations, with notes and commentaries, of both Persian and Urdu poems.

A few works dealing with individual aspects of Iqbal's thought may be mentioned. Bashir Ahmad Dar's *Iqbal and Post-Kantian Voluntarism* (Lahore: Bazm-i Iqbal, 1956) studies the Western background to the development of Iqbal's concept of *khudi* by comparing Iqbal with a number of Western thinkers and writers. K. G. Saiyidayn's *Educational Philosophy of Iqbal* (Lahore: Sh. Muhammad Ashraf, 4th edn. 1954; first published 1938) is a well-known classic; its synopsis met with Iqbal's approval. M. Ikram Chaghatai's *Iqbal and Goethe* (Iqbal Academy Pakistan, Lahore, 2000) is a collection of articles by various authors exploring aspects of an interesting subject. Khalid Mas'ud's *Iqbal's Reconstruction of Ijtihad* (Lahore: Iqbal Academy Pakistan; Islamabad: Islamic Research Institute, 1995) discusses in detail the sixth lecture ('The Principle of Movement in the Structure of Islam') of Iqbal's *Reconstruction*.

Index